A HARD CHOICE

Sexual Abstinence
IN AN OUT-OF-CONTROL WORLD

DR. JESÚS CRUZ CORREA
DR. DORIS COLÓN SANTIAGO

A HARD CHOICE

Sexual Abstinence
IN AN OUT-OF-CONTROL WORLD

DR. JESÚS CRUZ CORREA
DR. DORIS COLÓN SANTIAGO

About Photocopying This Book

1 Timothy 5:17-18 instructs us to give the laborer his wages, specifically those who labor in the Word and doctrine. Hensley Publishing has a moral, as well as legal responsibility to see that our authors receive fair compensation for their efforts. Many of them depend upon the income from the sale of their books as their sole livelihood. So, for that matter, do the artists, printers, and numerous other people who work to make these books available to you. Please help us by discouraging those who would copy this material in lieu of purchase.

Unless otherwise noted, Scripture references in this study are taken from the HOLY BIBLE, NEW INTERNATIONAL VERSION. Copyright © 1973, 1978, 1984 by International Bible Society. Used by permission of Zondervan Bible Publishers.

HENSLEY
PUBLISHING

ISBN 1-56322-080-6

A Hard Choice

Table of Contents

Acknowledgements

We wish to express our deepest gratitude to the Holy Spirit for His guidance and confirmation during the many months that were dedicated to the writing of this book. To our sons Cristóbal and Eduardo, who served as our inspiration, and as such we bless them and are thankful for their continuous words of encouragement.

We wish to thank brother Victor Cruz from Hensley Publishing, for being faithful to the leading of the Spirit, and to Terri Kalfas and her review board. You made this project a reality. Congratulations to Cristina Fernandez for her labor as the editor for the Spanish translation, and graphic designer.

We also wish to thank graphic artist Marvin Santiago, for his many hours of work with the book's illustrations, and to our brother Santos Torres for videotaping and editing some of the surgical procedures.

We must also recognize each of the young people who for the last five years have worked with us in our ministry travels and conferences. A special word of thanks to a very special person, a faithful supporter and the person in charge of videotaping all our conferences, Ruben Irizarry.

And last, but in no way the least, each young person who has served as our inspiration and given us the privilege to share with them about God's holiness and purity.

Introduction

The personal concept that I had concerning sexual abstinence among young people had been quite impersonal. This took a drastic change as I attended to an office full of patients in my OBGYN practice one particular day.

One of my patients, a 48-year-old woman had been in surgery for the removal of a benign tumor in her uterus, and came to the office for a follow-up visit, and to have some of the stitches that remained as a result of the operation removed. The lady asked me if I could please examine her 10-year-old daughter who was having sharp pains in her stomach, a possible symptom of appendicitis. I told her that I was not a pediatrician. But I decided to examine the young girl anyway. As I examined this 10-year-old girl who weighed no more than 77 pounds, I was shocked to discover that she was not having colic, or an appendicitis attack. She was four and one-half months pregnant.

How could it be possible that a mature woman, a mother, didn't realize that her daughter was four and one-half months pregnant? Even though I had performed more than two thousand deliveries in my practice as an obstetrician, this event made such an impact in my life that I began to do research in a small city in my country, Puerto Rico. I discovered that in 1995, in only one of the high schools in the city, there were ninety-three pregnant girls, under seventeen years of age.

As a man, a father, a Christian, a doctor and a U.S. citizen, I had to ask myself: Where have we failed? What haven't we done? When, and how, did our moral values turn upside down, to the extreme that more than forty-five percent of our teenagers, *including Christian teenagers*, have become sexually active?

Many years ago, the federal government began a program, through the Department of Education, entitled *Safe Sex*. The bathrooms of our schools were fitted with machines that dispensed condoms, and a humanist sexual education curriculum, absent of moral values, was implemented. The message is quite clear: The only thing that matters is to avoid getting pregnant or being infected by AIDS.

Many years after this futile attempt, we observed, as expected, a debacle in moral and health problems. The statistics revealed that new births, venereal diseases, abortions and the use of pornography had all increased by two hundred percent.

As doctors, we are very close to issues of life and death. We have shared in the joy of our patients as they receive into the world a new creature who will fill their parents' lives with great happiness. At the same time, we have experienced great sadness when a baby dies during delivery.

God, in His great love, has bestowed upon us the right of sexual expression. He has given us human beings the physical, emotional and spiritual ability to love and procreate. But it must be done exclusively within the holy bond of marriage. When we violate this precept with aberrant and pre-marital sexual practices, resulting in unwanted pregnancies and venereal diseases, we twist God's divine purpose and suffer the consequences.

> As a man, a father, a Christian, a doctor and a U.S. citizen, I had to ask myself: Where have we failed? What haven't we done? When and how did our moral values turn upside down, to the extreme that more than forty-five percent of our teenagers, *including Christian teenagers,* have become sexually active?

We recognize that in the last one hundred years, no other generation has been under such pressure to give in to offers of promiscuity, lewdness and lascivious behavior, pornography, divorce, drugs, moral and spiritual decadence, the occult, mental disorders and suicide among teenagers. Never before, have mass media and other means of communication, commerce, the movie industry and the internet turned sex into its main source of publicity and income.

More than two thousand years ago, the Word of God described sexual abstinence as the only effective solution to this great dilemma. The Bible does not change — it forever remains the same. It was given unto men to protect their lives and save their souls. This is the reason my wife, Doris, and I have no doubt whatsoever that this message of sexual abstinence comes directly from the heart of God, and is God's will for these difficult times in which we live. Our experiences as believers, as doctors and as parents have led us to officially organize the ministry *Waiting for True Love.* Through this ministry we have been able to minister to more than 72,000 young people.

We have called upon the Holy Spirit to speak in a very special way, and to awaken the heart of teenagers, parents, singles, church councils, religious denominations, pastors, leaders, educators, health professionals and government officials to — and make them painfully aware of — the seriousness, gravity and urgency of bringing to the forefront a message like this with its life and death implications.

We pray that God, in His mercy, will begin a work of restoration in the lives of those who have fallen prey to Satan's lies and worldly practices; teach and guide all adolescents in matters of their sexuality; and make it possible for government officials, parents, educators, medical doctors and the local churches to use the tools He has already provided, in order to speak to young people about sex. As a result, single men and women should be able to live in any stage of their lives with a pattern of reference that is holy and pure, as ordained and required by God.

More than two thousand years ago, the Word of God described sexual abstinence as the only effective solution to this great dilemma. The Bible does not change — it forever remains the same.

PART ONE

Lesson 1

Waiting for True Love: The Heart of God

From behind the curtains we could hear the voices of more than 1,000 students who had filled the theater. We were about to begin, and there was a great deal of nervous activity going on behind the stage, where more than 60 young volunteers and members of our production team, musicians, stage hands, ushers and other volunteers had gathered to participate in the first city-wide youth rally of the *Waiting for True Love* ministry.

After praying with all the staff members, going over the program outline one last time, and listening to the voice of my wife as she gave final instructions over the intercom, I felt the need to be alone with the Lord and sought a dark corner behind the stage. It was the month of April 1995, three months after I had diagnosed the unsuspected pregnancy of my patient's ten-year-old child. There were so many things to pray for at that moment... but the voice of the Spirit brought to my mind the following verse:

> *In the same way, the Spirit helps us in our weakness. We do not know what we ought to pray for, but the Spirit himself intercedes for us.*
> —Romans 8:26

This calmed me down and allowed me to enjoy those brief moments alone with God. The Lord brought to memory the vision he had shown me two months before. It happened during a particular morning when I was already awake. I clearly saw a great multitude of students from the public school system walking into a great auditorium, and immediately I knew that it was not a church setting. I received the conviction that it would take place in the *La Perla Theater*, in the city of Ponce, Puerto Rico.

God's Faithfulness

God is faithful, and two months later I found myself in this very theater, ready to communicate God's message of sexual abstinence to more than 1,000 students. The words found in Ephesians 3:20 had become a reality. Hundreds of young people screamed in unison as the master of ceremonies called the name of each school present. This brought me back to reality and made me

The word of God is living and active. Sharper than any double-edged sword, it penetrates even to dividing soul and spirit, joints and marrow; it judges the thoughts and attitudes of the heart.
—Hebrews 4:12

realize that the first of many Student Rallies of *Waiting for True Love*, had just begun.

Sensitive to God's Voice

One more time I reviewed the plan God had shown me: the script for each sketch, the need to encourage the student-led musical team, the need to be dynamic and original, but above all, sincere and transparent with the truth we were about to share with these young people. We had to captivate their attention, and make them understand that the message of sexual abstinence is a life and death message.

The music team closed the first part of the program. The young crowd fully identified with them, with their sound and with the biblical message that was sung in a language and style they could understand. Everything was beginning to produce the desired effect. They were all paying attention.

The Challenge

As medical doctors, we had participated in conferences and seminars at all levels of our expertise. A Christians, we had preached the Word of God in many places, but now we faced a great challenge: to teach these young people God's point of view about their sexuality, and to be instrumental in helping them make the decision to sign and commit to an abstinence covenant that would protect their lives and be pleasing unto God.

Thanks to the intervention of the Holy Spirit, we were able to explain how God created them with the need for affection and intimacy. We taught them about the anatomy of their reproductive organs, the process of delivery, peer pressure, STD's and abortion with its damaging consequences. We presented sexual abstinence as the only alternative that God offers in order to arrive at their wedding physically, emotionally and spiritually pure and healthy.

God Honors His Promises

Two and a half hours had gone by, and the presence of God was so real. The students' respectful attitude and attention was at a maximum. The only interruptions came when occasionally they would break out in cries of amazement and unbelief as real scenes of a baby being delivered, pictures of a real abortion and C-sections flashed across the giant movie screen.

Now to him who is able to do immeasurably more than all we ask or imagine, according to his power that is at work within us.
—Ephesians 3:20

We presented sexual abstinence as the only alternative that God offers in order to arrive at their wedding physically, emotionally and spiritually pure and healthy.

Finally, the time to sign the Abstinence Covenant had arrived. Our eyes were filled with tears when we observed that more than ninety percent of all the students present were placing their signatures on the covenant certificates. Most raised their hands as a sign of having prayed to receive Jesus into their hearts for the very first time, as the only way possible to fully carry out the covenant made. We understood that God wanted to start a special movement of His Spirit among the youth of our country, Puerto Rico, and we took this answer to prayer as a sign.

The Reality of God's Word

Over and over again we have been able to prove that when young people are exposed to the truth, the answer doesn't tarry — even though they may have been bombarded by the media's attempt to spoil God's perfect plan. Deep within our beings, God has sowed the need for purity.

> These past few years God allowed us to see that same response: Young people who are being impacted by the truth, and who have fully recognized the value of their sexuality.

Doris and I have asked God to allow us to dream without boundaries, in order to proclaim God's calling to holiness and to sexual abstinence along with an army of young and single people throughout the world. We need radical people who are willing to prepare the way for the return of Jesus Christ, our Lord.

As we read through this book and study God's Word, the Holy Spirit will teach us that sexual abstinence is the lifestyle of purity and holiness that God requires outside of marriage.

These past few years God allowed us to see that same response: Young people who are being impacted by the truth, and who have fully recognized the value of their sexuality.

Let's search the Scriptures. Read the following verses. Meditate upon them and make a note of the biblical principle found in the Word of God:

Matthew 5:18

_____
_____
_____
_____

Matthew 24:35

_____

_____

_____

Isaiah 40:7-8

_____

_____

_____

The Word of God is our only source of truth. Our arguments will be based only on the Word.

Psalm 119:89-91

_____

_____

_____

Isaiah 55:10-11

_____

_____

_____

The Word of God is our only source of truth. Our arguments must be based only on the Word. What is the main biblical principle for the previous verses?

_____

_____

_____

_____

What is our only source of information for this study?

_____

_____

Why must we use the Word as the only source of truth?

_____

_____

_____

We have previously stated that God's message for young people is a message of life or death. We must urgently recognize that many times the life of our young people depends on a fine line that separates holiness from sin, life from death. Life, when we obey God's commandment to avoid sin, to preserve the purity of our own bodies, to abstain from sexual relations outside of marriage. And death, spiritual or physical, when we decide to follow after our own desires and disobey the Word of God.

In certain hospitals where a specific area has been designated for patients who are suffering from AIDS, it's eye-opening to observe how infrequently patients are visited by friends and families. Among the visitors you will never find that particular "friend" who involved these patients in the use of illicit drugs for the very first time; you will not find that person who was responsible for infecting them, or the person who seduced them into having sexual relations which resulted in them contracting this disease.

During the summer of 1996, I was called to the emergency room to see Antonia, a 21-year-old patient suffering from AIDS. On this particular occasion she was suffering from bilateral pneumonia, and her overall condition was quite poor. She had been contaminated by her boyfriend, a very elegant young man with whom she was sexually involved. Antonia, my patient, had no prior knowledge that this handsome young man with the great hair and striking blue eyes, was a drug addict who also had the AIDS virus. She could not see beyond the athletic appearance and the fact that he was employed by a banking institution.

Along with a specialist in internal medicine, I made the decision to admit Antonia. For the next forty-eight days, we watched as this beautiful and happy young woman developed a fungal infection all over her mouth and throughout her digestive system, and her body became covered with violet-colored spots (Sarcoma de Kaposi). Since her lungs were invaded by the fatal bacteria Pneumocytis Carinii, she finally died in her mother's arms, following a massive brain hemorrhage which produced convulsions and a cardio-respiratory (heart and lung) arrest.

Antonia was not the only one to die. One year later her two-year-old son also died; he was contaminated with the AIDS virus when he was in his mothers womb, without her ever suspecting any of it.

In certain hospitals where a specific area has been designated for patients who are suffering from AIDS, it's eye-opening to observe how infrequently patients are visited by friends and families. Among the visitors you will never find that particular "friend" who involved these patients in the use of illicit drugs for the very first time; you will not find that person who is responsible for infecting them or the person who seduced them into having sexual relations which resulted in them contracting this disease.

In just this instance, not recognizing or having respect for the principle of sexual abstinence produced a total of three deaths that could be accounted for statistically. This number includes Antonia's boyfriend who also died; but it doesn't include all the other women who were contaminated by this man before he died, victims of the sin of fornication and of disobeying God's commandment concerning sexual abstinence.

Read and analyze the following verses, then answer the questions:

Genesis 2:16-17
What quality of our forefathers did the Lord wish to prove with this order?

_____

_____

Not recognizing or having respect for the principle of sexual abstinence produced a total of three deaths that could be accounted for statistically.

To what type of death is God referring in His warning?

_____

_____

In Deuteronomy 30:15-16; 19-20, what is God's promise in exchange for our holiness and obedience?

_____

_____

Write down the two main attributes of God.
1._____
2._____

Read Jeremiah 21:8. Which are the two ways God is offering to us?
1._____
2._____

Not recognizing or having respect for the principle of sexual abstinence produced a total of three deaths that could be accounted for statistically.

Tell the people, This is what the LORD says: "See, I am setting before you the way of life and the way of death."
—Jeremiah 21:8

Why does sexual abstinence offers us "the way of life"?

_____

_____

_____

_____

What is the difference between physical death and eternal death?

_____

_____

Write down and analyze the following verses:

John 8:51

_____

_____

_____

What is the importance of keeping and obeying the Word of God?

_____

_____

_____

My son, pay attention to what I say; listen closely to my words. Do not let them out of your sight, keep them within your heart; for they are life to those who find them and health to a man's whole body. Above all else, guard your heart, for it is the wellspring of life.
—*Proverbs 4:20-23*

Proverbs 4:20-23

_____

_____

Write 3 reasons why sexual abstinence could represent life for the one who practices it.

1._____

2._____

3._____

In what way can the Word of God be "health (medicine) to our bodies"?
Proverbs 8:34-36

_____

_____

What is the way to pleasing God? Why?

_____

_____

_____

What is the sensible thing to do if your wish is to live safely and wisely?

_____

_____

What are the 2 major attributes of God? How do these preserve life when we obey them?

_____

_____

Write Proverb 11:19

_____

_____

_____

List the 5 principal causes of death among young people today.

1._____

2._____

3._____

4._____

5._____

Which commandment of the Word of God is violated by each of these?

_____

_____

Give 3 reasons why sexual abstinence before marriage brings life or death.

1._____

2._____

3._____

In the Bible, sexual abstinence is the only alternative recognized by God that is able to deliver us from spiritual death, and even the physical death, that is produced by sexual sins. It keeps us pure for the partner that He has destined as our companion for the rest of our lives.

The season of our youth is part of His divine plan for our lives. God gave it to us so that we might enjoy it fully, within the boundaries of holiness and purity. As we walk in His Word, we can know the dimensions of freedom, peace and joy that God gives during this season of our lives, thus avoiding the pain that fatal consequences can and will provoke as a result of our ignorance and disobedience.

Millie, a young 22-year-old business administration senior, and a believer, came to my office because of a hormonal imbalance. During the initial examination she confessed that she was not a virgin, and had on only one occasion had sexual relations with her boyfriend. When asked why she did it, she lowered her eyes and said she regretted it: "Even though my wedding is only six months away, I don't have anything to look forward to. I've lost the excitement, the anticipation of being with my new husband for the first time on my wedding night. It will never be the same; and even though I have repented of my sin, we can't turn back time."

Answer the following questions in light of Romans 6:23.

What type of death is referred to as the result of "the wages of sin."?

_____

_____

_____

What is the difference between physical and spiritual death?

_____

_____

_____

In the Bible, sexual abstinence is the only alternative recognized by God to deliver us from spiritual death, and even the physical death, that is produced by sexual sins.

What is a gift?

_____

_____

Who is the only one who can give the gift of eternal life? Why?

_____

_____

_____

What is the means for acquiring eternal life?

_____

_____

_____

The answer to the spiritual death that we inherited from our forefathers is found in God's plan of salvation through His Son Jesus.

Write the verse found in Romans 8:1-2

_____

_____

_____

What is the necessary requirement that must be present in order for divine justice to be applied to our lives?

_____

_____

_____

How are we delivered from the law of sin and death?

_____

_____

_____

The wages of sin is death, but the gift of God is eternal life in Christ Jesus our Lord.
—Romans 6:23

Write the verse found in John 14:6

_____

_____

_____

Which is the only way to come to the Father?

_____

_____

What promise is fulfilled when we decide to travel this road?

_____

_____

_____

Jesus is the Word of God, and if we decide to travel the way of His Word, then we must know Jesus. If you don't know Him yet, personally, then invite Him to come into your heart as your Lord and Savior. When you have reached the end of this study, if there is a feeling of emptiness in your heart and a deep desire to repent of your sins, it's because the Spirit of God is calling you. Close your eyes for a brief moment, and tell God that you don't want one more religion, but a life relationship with Him. Remember that obedience to His Word can only be accomplished through Him.

Jesus is the Word of God, and if we decide to travel the road of His Word, then we must know Jesus.

Read the following prayer aloud:

> ***Lord Jesus, I confess that I am a sinner. Please forgive all my sins. Come and dwell in my heart as my Lord and my Savior. Amen.***

Lesson 2

Getting to Know Your Own Body

Once again, the Spirit of God manifested Himself in a very special way; this particular day it was in the Patria theater in Bogotá Colombia. That morning the theater was filled beyond capacity by more than 1,200 students, and the afternoon session proved to be the same. School buses brought students from every neighborhood in the city. This multi-media presentation of *Waiting for True Love* in Bogotá had been well organized. More than 4,200 students heard the message.

At the end of the event, the production personnel, actors and musicians were all acknowledged by the students and their teachers with a well-deserved ovation. There was an enormous sense of thankfulness, and sincere enthusiasm in the air. You could almost touch it. These students had learned the truth about their sexuality, and a real description of how their bodies function. We made it very clear that God, the Creator of our body, demands that every sexual relation must be limited to the holy bond of matrimony.

Because we knew that many of the students present in each session were sexually active, we spoke of a forgiving God who welcomes us with open arms when we come to Him in repentance and express our desire for a brand new start.

We told them about a second virginity which takes place when we truly repent, and that God forgives us and we begin a life of sexual abstinence, a life in which we experience emotional and spiritual healing. We explained that we must place our trust in God's faithfulness to provide that person He has chosen for us, someone who will love, understand and accept us as we are.

When I stepped down from the stage, a group of young ladies was waiting to express their gratitude and request that we sign their notebooks. One of the young ladies, in the latter stage of pregnancy, mentioned how impressed she was with the visuals of a baby being delivered, something she would soon have to experience at such an early age. Some expressed their doubts and fears, and asked us to sign the Abstinence Covenant we had given them.

Flee from sexual immorality. All other sins a man commits are outside his body, but he who sins sexually sins against his own body. Do you not know that your body is a temple of the Holy Spirit, who is in you, whom you have received from God? You are not your own; you were bought at a price. Therefore honor God with your body.
—1 Corinthians 6:18-20

A 13-year-old girl pulled me aside and told me that her boyfriend constantly pressured her to have sexual relations with him. All of his previous girlfriends had done it. The only reason she had refused was because she believed she was too young. It was obvious that until this moment she had been unaware, or hadn't wanted to recognize God's warnings concerning sex outside marriage.

It was very moving for me to hear her say that now she knew that sex before marriage was a sin, and that she could not participate in sexual relations until her wedding day. And with a gesture that was typical of her age, she emphatically said that if her boyfriend refused to see things her way, she would end the relationship.

Hearing the comments made by this young girl gave me the satisfaction of knowing that God's purpose had been fulfilled that day in that theater. Her testimony was gratifying; the Holy Spirit had caused her to understand the truth.

Basic Principles of the Anatomy of the Reproductive System

We are the maximum expression of God's creation. The human body was designed with a very special touch. No human being knows the intimate secrets of life and death, only the Creator does.

In dealing with life and illnesses in the human being, we medical doctors can only apply those scientific principles which God has already revealed. God is the giver of life, and only He takes it away.

From an early age, children develop a certain curiosity about their own body. The reproductive system is an integral part of who a person is. That needs to be recognized, studied, understood and explained as if it were the most natural thing in the world, because such knowledge about the body plays a very important role in the emotional stability of a young person during puberty and sexual development.

1—THE FEMALE REPRODUCTIVE SYSTEM

The woman's reproductive system is located at the center of the feminine pelvis, protected by the two "coxales" bones and the sacrum and coccix bones in the rear. These bones are surrounded by a complex network of muscles, ligaments and tendons. (See figures 1 and 2.)

Uterus: The uterus, an organ shaped like an inverted pear, is composed of muscle fibers. In the adult woman it weighs approximately two ounces and measures three inches in length. Its interior cavity is lined with a specialized membrane called endometrio. It's in this cavity that the fetus is sheltered and grows, and it's the place from where the blood flow that is produced with menstruation proceeds. The uterus shares its space with the bladder on the upper region and with the rectum (the last portion of the large intestine) in the lower region.

Fallopian tubes: Located on both the lateral and superior parts of the uterus, these two structures made of muscle and fiber look like arms approximately four inches long. Their principal function is to collect the sperm and the egg that is released from the ovary during the period of ovulation, which normally occurs usually 14 days after the first day of menstruation. In its travel through this tube is where the sperm (male reproductive cell) unites with the egg and fertilization occurs, or a new life begins.

Ovaries: The ovaries are two egg-shaped structures that measure one and one half inches long and three-fourths of an inch wide. This is where the eggs, or feminine reproductive cells, are formed. At the time of the first menstruation, the ovaries house nearly 400,000 eggs which will be used, generally speaking at a rate of one per month, throughout the life of the ovary's reproductive life.

Vagina: The vagina is an organ made of fiber and muscle, which connects the external part, or vulva, with the cervix. This is the channel through which the baby descends during birth. The bladder is located in the upper region.

The organs of the female reproductive system are the uterus, fallopian tubes, ovaries, vagina and vulva.

The organs of the female reproductive system are the uterus, fallopian tubes, ovaries, vagina and vulva.

2—THE MALE REPRODUCTIVE SYSTEM

The male reproductive system is lodged in the pelvis. Its external region is formed by: scrotal sacks, testicles, epididymis, vas deferens, prostate, seminal vesicle, and the penis.

Scrotal sacks Two oval structures in the form of a sack that hold both testicles (male reproductive glands). They help maintain an optimal temperature in order to preserve the sperm.

Testicles: The testicles are the oval-shaped structures in charge of producing sperm and male hormones. These are connected to the vas deferens in order to carry the sperm to the penis. (Figure 5).

The organs of the male reproductive system are: scrotal sacks, testicles, vas deferens, prostate, seminal vesicle, and penis.

Vas deferens: The vas deferens is an elongated tube through which the sperm travel until they reach the penis. It can easily be felt through the skin of the scrotal sacks. During a vasectomy procedure (male sterilization) these are cut and/or cauterized.

Prostate: This gland produces the liquid that activates the sperm so they can flow. It is found beneath the bladder.

Seminal vesicle: This is a gland located beneath the bladder and near the prostate, which produces the liquid that transports and releases the sperm. This liquid provides fructose and other substances that feed the sperm and improve its capacity to fertilize.

Penis: Along with the scrotal sacks, the penis forms the external genital organs of the male. It is designed for copulation (sexual relations for procreation) and to deposit the sperm in the vagina of the female. Internally it communicates with the bladder and also serves as an organ of excretion. On the inside it has hollow spaces which are filled with blood and produce the erection in the male during sexual relations.

Let's search the Scriptures.
God has created us as tripartite (three part) beings. Which are the parts that make us who we are?

1 Thessalonians 5:23

_____

_____

_____

Man is a being made up of spirit, soul and body. Within this being are three elements that are interrelated. Answer the following questions and fill the blank spaces:

1. The place where hate is originated _____.

2. The _____ is the seat of our emotions.

3. Is in direct communion with God: _____.

4. The _____ has control over our will.

Hebrews 4:12 explains the way in which the Word of God acts upon our whole being. Describe it in your own words.

_____

_____

_____

Write the verse found in Romans 8:11.

_____

_____

_____

Mass media has transformed the worship and idolatry of the body into an extremely lucrative business in which billions are invested.

According to Romans 8:11, what is the requirement in order for us to be raised with the Lord at the time of His return? Please explain.

_____

_____

_____

How will our mortal bodies be transformed into immortal ones?

_____

_____

_____

Mass media has transformed the worship and idolatry of the body into an extremely lucrative business in which billions are invested. There is an avalanche of plastic surgery recommendations, exercise programs, diets, vitamins and dietetic supplements, the famous "day spas," meditation and mental wellness camps… and much, much more.

As medical doctors we recommend and counsel patients in the care of their bodies, with the appropriate motivation. As Christians, we preach that we are the temple of the Holy Spirit.

Write the verse found in Genesis 2:7.

_____

_____

_____

What elements did God use to give us life?

_____

_____

_____

The LORD God formed the man from the dust of the ground and breathed into his nostrils the breath of life, and the man became a living being.
—Genesis 2:7

What makes us different from everything else God created?

_____

_____

_____

Write down the following verses and analyze how we were created by God.
Genesis 1:26-27

_____

_____

_____

_____

Genesis 2:7

_____

_____

_____

_____

Psalm 103:14

_____

_____

_____

_____

Job 33:4

_____

_____

_____

_____

Psalm 51:5

_____

_____

_____

_____

Despite our physical frailty, we are complex beings which only God, our Creator, can fully understand to the final detail. God ministers separately to every aspect of our lives and teaches us to recognize our fallen nature and our redeemed nature.

Read the following verses and describe in your words why God created you. What purpose and what responsibility does He have for your life?

Psalm 139:13-16

_____

_____

_____

_____

Psalm 119:73

_____

_____

_____

_____

God ministers separately to every aspect of our lives and teaches us to recognize our fallen nature and our redeemed nature.

Job 10:11-12

_____

_____

_____

_____

In His infinite love toward man, God became man, and took the shape of a servant so that everyone who believes in Him will be saved and have eternal life. In order to show us His love and mercy, He took the same human body He had designed for us. Knowing its weaknesses and limitations, He suffered for our sins in His own flesh.

Write the verse found in Philippians 2:5-11 and answer the following questions.

_____

_____

_____

_____

_____

> There is no doubt that God knows perfectly the weaknesses and temptations of our bodies; He created us and also experienced them in His own flesh, but was without sin.

What motivated the Lord to empty Himself of His divine nature and choose our human form?

_____

_____

_____

What did it mean for Him to empty Himself of His divine nature?

_____

_____

_____

For what kind of a crime was death on a cross reserved?

_____

_____

_____

Therefore, there is no doubt that God knows perfectly the weaknesses and temptations of our bodies; He created us and also experienced them in His own flesh, but was without sin. In the Old Testament, the high priest could enter into the Holy of Holies only once a year, with the purpose of making atonement for his own and for the sins of the people. Yet despite such a privileged position, he was unable to know or understand the weaknesses or sins of each person.

Analyze Hebrews 4:15 and list 5 basic differences between the Old and the New Testament concerning the atonement of sins:

1._____
2._____
3._____
4._____
5._____

In the Word of God there are many serious warnings concerning what happens when we reject God's counsel and do not submit our bodies to the obedience of the Holy Spirit. When we surrender our bodies and our minds to sinning, wickedness begins to erode our conscience. God allows us to choose freely, to the point of losing our ability to recognize the sin that seduces and enslaves us. Read the story of Lot and his family in Genesis 19:1-38, and answer the following questions.

Therefore God gave them over in the sinful desires of their hearts to sexual impurity for the degrading of their bodies with one another.
—Romans 1:24

What motivated Lot to move each day closer and closer to Sodom, a place full of so much evil?

_____
_____
_____
_____
_____
_____

Lot's wife looked back, and she became a pillar of salt.
—Genesis 19:26

What type of sins characterized that city?

_____
_____
_____
_____
_____

In Genesis chapter 18, Abraham interceded before God on behalf of the city.

Explain why God could not exercise His mercy over this city.

_____

_____

_____

_____

_____

Furthermore, since they did not think it worthwhile to retain the knowledge of God, he gave them over to a depraved mind, to do what ought not to be done.
—Romans 1:28

Explain the degree of depravity in which the city found itself when they asked Lot to hand over the two men that were visiting his home.

_____

_____

_____

_____

Why did Lot's wife turn into a pillar of salt?

_____

_____

_____

_____

_____

What could have motivated Lot's wife to make such a decision?

_____

_____

_____

_____

_____

Sin affects our capacity to reason and discern between good and evil. There are families in which a determined pattern of sins is practiced: adultery, divorce, alcoholism, crime, sexual immorality, rape, abuse etc. The story of Lot is a classic example of how much sin can capture the mind of a person or family, making it impossible for them to discern between good and evil and thus have no control over the use of their bodies.

Write Genesis 19:36:

_____

_____

_____

_____

_____

Why did Lot's daughters wish to have descendants with their own father?

_____

_____

_____

_____

_____

What were the consequences suffered by the people of Israel as the result of the sin of incest by Lot's daughters?

_____

_____

_____

_____

In the book of Romans, the apostle Paul emphasizes the radical treatment of sin. Write the verse found in Romans 12:1-2.

_____

_____

_____

_____

How are we to treat our bodies in the process of transformation?

_____

_____

_____

_____

Those who live according to the sinful nature have their minds set on what that nature desires; but those who live in accordance with the Spirit have their minds set on what the Spirit desires.
—Romans 8:5-7

How do we present our own bodies as a living sacrifice?

_____

_____

_____

_____

_____

The Word of God lasts forever. What does the apostle Paul mean when he recommends that we not conform to the patterns of this world?

_____

_____

_____

_____

To what group of people is Paul referring to when he speaks of those "who live according to the sinful nature"?

_____

_____

_____

_____

_____

Do you not know that your body is a temple of the Holy Spirit, who is in you, whom you have received from God? You are not your own; you were bought at a price. Therefore honor God with your body.
—1 Corinthians 6:19-20

What is the main difference between one group and the other?

_____

_____

_____

_____

Read Galatians 5:19-21 and list the works of the flesh (or body).

_____

_____

_____

_____

The will of God is for us to be pure inside and outside, because we have been washed by the blood of Christ and sealed with the Holy Spirit.

Read 1 Corinthians 6:19-20 and answer the following questions:

When does the Holy Spirit come to make his dwelling in our lives?

_____

_____

_____

_____

It is God's will that you should be sanctified: that you should avoid sexual immorality.
—1 Thessalonians 4:3

Explain why the apostle affirms that we do not belong to ourselves.

_____

_____

_____

_____

_____

Explain in your own words the relationship of the body with sanctification.

_____

_____

_____

_____

_____

How would you explain to your own son /daughter the concept of the body as an instrument of sin?

_____

_____

_____

The Word says that we are members of the Body of Christ, and that we ought to live as worthy of such a high calling, including sexual purity. It also describes with wisdom and divine eloquence that God is the great Architect of a great temple which has Christ as the cornerstone and ourselves as the living stones of this spiritual house and holy priesthood. The Church is the Body of Christ, his bride, and like every bride it must arrive at her wedding pure and without blemish.

Meditate on the following verses and write the main idea.

1 Peter 2:4-9

_____
_____
_____
_____
_____
_____

Ephesians 2:19-22

_____
_____
_____
_____
_____
_____

1 Corinthians 12:12-14

_____
_____
_____
_____
_____

Once you were alienated from God and were enemies in your minds because of your evil behavior. But now he has reconciled you by Christ's physical body through death to present you holy in his sight, without blemish and free from accusation.
—Colossians 1:21-22

Ephesians 4:1-6, 16

_____
_____
_____
_____

Ephesians 5:25-27

_____
_____
_____
_____
_____
_____

Colossians 1:21-22

_____

_____

_____

_____

_____

_____

Revelation 14:4-5

_____

_____

_____

_____

_____

_____

In a brief summary explain the following: How does God want us to treat our bodies? What is the purpose of your body? What are the consequences for disobeying His commandments?

_____

_____

_____

_____

_____

_____

_____

_____

Lesson 3

The Miracle of Reproduction

As it was always our custom following the morning surgical procedures, we headed for the office in order to see the patients who had been scheduled for the afternoon. It had been two years since Rosa's last visit to the office, but after one look at her I could easily detect that something was wrong. She was only 14 years old. She came accompanied by her mother, who told me that Rosa was suffering from high blood pressure, swollen legs and ankles, and kidney complications.

When Rosa had been 12 years old she experienced complications in the 6th month of pregnancy. Without a doubt she was a high-risk patient, so we had referred her to a specialized hospital in order to for her to receive the appropriate treatment she deserved. During her 8th month of pregnancy, she developed toxemia. The symptoms consist of a massive loss of proteins in the urine, swelling of the whole body, increase in blood pressure, and in the worst of cases, convulsions resembling epilepsy that place the life of the patient and her baby in great danger. This is a condition observed in first-time pregnancies, in which the younger the patient the more serious the complications.

After giving birth to her child, Rosa remained hospitalized in the intensive care unit because of the convulsions she experienced and because her kidneys had been gravely affected. Age 12 is not the appropriate time for any girl to get pregnant. When children give birth to children, the body is not mature enough to handle the great changes and risks that a woman goes through during pregnancy, delivery and post-delivery. Sexual abstinence was the protection that Rosa needed.

After the birth of her child I had not heard from Rosa again, so now I asked her about the baby, and if he was walking yet. Without a hint of emotion or any expression of life she revealed the sad truth that her baby had died at eight months of age due to various health complications.

What happened to Rosa is one more example of what happens when the Word of God is violated. At a very early age she lived and suffered the consequences

God blessed them and said to them, "Be fruitful and increase in number; fill the earth and subdue it...."
—*Genesis 1:28*

Age 12 is not the appropriate time for any girl to get pregnant.

of her disobedience and ignorance. In most cases, young people are the victims of lack of instruction, or lack of the right kind of information. We are all to blame: the system of education, parents, the church and mass media. I pray to the Holy Spirit that everyone who reads this book will be enlightened concerning the seriousness and urgency of this matter. To know, to teach, to inform and to accept what God says about our sexuality and holiness, is a matter of life and death.

The Mechanism of Reproduction

1—CONCEPTION

Conception is the fertilization of an egg by the sperm. It takes place in the first half of the fallopian tubes, once the sperm and the egg unite. These two cells multiply rather quickly, and in approximately 3 or 4 days they travel through the fallopian tubes and reach the rear part of the uterine cavity. It is here that during the next 9 months, or 40 weeks, the baby will develop each of its systems and organs (Illustration 4).

2—DELIVERY

> *Can you fathom the mysteries of God? Can you probe the limits of the Almighty? They are higher than the heavens — what can you do? Their measure is longer than the earth and wider than the sea.*
> *—Job 11:7-9*

In God's perfect timing, a series of contractions begin in the muscular fiber of the uterus, and continue to grow in intensity, duration and consistency in order to allow the cervix to progressively dilate and for the child to accommodate himself in the vaginal canal, until the child is finally delivered. The beginning of the contractions and preparation of the uterus is attributed to substances called prostaglandins.

Childbirth is a continuous process that has been divided into three stages:

First Stage — DILATION: The period of time between the beginning of the contractions and the full dilation of the cervix.

Second Stage — EXPULSION: The period of time between the complete dilation of the cervix until the expulsion of the baby through the vaginal canal.

Third Stage — BIRTH: The period of time between the birth of the baby until the expulsion of the placenta.

Sometimes a baby cannot be born through the mother's vaginal canal. When this happens, it is necessary to perform a cesarean section. A C-Section (Illustration 13) is the surgical procedure by which the baby is extracted through an incision made in the mother's abdomen and womb. Some of the conditions that necessitate that a C-section be performed are:

• Wrong Presentations: Any position of the child during childbirth other than head first; in other words bottom first, feet first, face first or sideways.

• Severe bleeding (hemorrhage) due to problems with the placenta, with the blood, or any other type of trauma, such as a car accident.

• Toxemia: The accumulation of body fluids, swelling, high blood pressure, and proteins in the urine.

• Vaginal contamination from venereal diseases, which at the time of delivery presents a high risk to the health of the child who can be contaminated as it passes through the vaginal canal. Examples are vaginal herpes type II (Illustration 8), or venereal warts (virus of the human papiloma) (Illustration 9).

• Narrow pelvis

• Multiple births: twins, triplets, Siamese twins, etc.

• Fetus stress due to lack of appropriate oxygen amounts.

Let's search the Scriptures and see what they say about this miracle of reproduction. God perpetuates life through the creative miracle of conception and the process of childbirth. He emptied Himself of His divinity and took on the body of a man in order to come into this world. He used the womb of a virgin who conceived by the power of the Holy Spirit to give life to the Son of God.

The Word became flesh and made his dwelling among us. We have seen his glory, the glory of the One and Only, who came from the Father, full of grace and truth.
—John 1:14

List and discuss in your own words the divine attributes found in this verse.

_____
_____
_____

Which supernatural events had to occur in order for this word to become a reality?

_____
_____
_____

How would you explain this event to an 8-year-old-child?

_____

_____

_____

_____

Having children is a privilege that God, in His divine plan, gives us in order for the reproduction of the human race to take place.

Explain why the psalmist compares children to a heritage.

_____

_____

_____

_____

In David's times, the warrior had to make his own arrows — he had to choose the best wood, resistant and lacking in humidity, and one as straight as possible in order to hit the mark. His very life depended upon this careful and detailed process.

How is this process compared with the process of having children?

_____

_____

_____

Why are there blessings in having children?

_____

_____

_____

Write the following verses and answer the following questions.
Genesis 33:5

_____

_____

_____

Deuteronomy 28:4

_____

_____

Sons are a heritage from the LORD, children a reward from him. Like arrows in the hands of a warrior are sons born in one's youth. Blessed is the man whose quiver is full of them.
—Psalm 127:3-5

Who blesses the fruit of our womb?

_____

_____

Mention 3 key events that occurred in order for God's promises to the Hebrew people to be fulfilled through the sons of Jacob.

1._____

2._____

3._____

Read Luke 1:26-38 and analyze the reaction of Mary's — Jesus' mother — when she was commissioned to carry the Son of God in her womb. List the fruits of the Spirit evident in Mary's life. (Also refer to Galatians 5:22-23.)

_____

_____

_____

Jesus replied, "What is impossible with men is possible with God."
—Luke 18:27

Name 3 women in the Bible who received a prophetic word or divine visitation before conceiving their child. Write the verses.

1._____

2._____

3._____

In which of the verses that we are studying can we apply the truth found in Luke 18:27?

_____

_____

_____

_____

What immediate and future consequences came about as the result of Mary's act of obedience?

_____

_____

_____

_____

_____

How do you compare Mary's faith with Zechariah's answer to the angel in Luke 1:18-20?

_____

_____

_____

_____

Are you ready to respond in the same way to a calling from God for your life? Explain.

_____

_____

_____

_____

"I am the Lord's servant,"
Mary answered. "May it
be to me as you have
said."
—Luke 1:38

The world, and man's fallen nature join forces to seduce young people. Each day that goes by, the statistics seem to be getting closer to the moment in which fifty percent or more of people under 18 years of age will be sexually active. That which God once blessed and said, "It is good," has been transformed and disfigured to the extent of making maternity seem like an insult.

Sadly, it is becoming more common to hear news of newborn babies that have been abandoned — usually by adolescent mothers. The chain of this curse frequently begins with children of unwed mothers — most of them belong to the poor sectors of society and are raised without care and love. These children have less opportunity to study and develop adequately, as compared with the other children their same age in other social contexts. The resulting lack of moral values, self-esteem and personal dignity all reflect the deep scars present from birth.

That which God once blessed and said, "It is good," has been transformed and disfigured to the extent of making maternity seem like an insult.

A couple from a neighborhood in the outskirts of the city where I reside had been waiting for me in my office since early that morning. Both tried in vain to hide the sadness that was evident in their faces. It was quite easy to detect that something was terribly wrong. The man began to talk, and went right to the point. His 14-year-old daughter — who was waiting outside — was pregnant.

After a pause, and obviously struggling with his words, the father said: "Doctor, my daughter is pregnant, and my 17 year old son is the father." Both parents began to cry under the weight of their shame, deep pain and the difficult situation they were facing. I was even more surprised when they requested that I perform an abortion on their daughter. They had confused my office with the office of an abortionist a few blocks away. I tried to convince them that despite the unfortunate circumstance they were facing, their decision to abort was a crime. All my efforts were in vain. They excused themselves and walked alongside their daughter to the abortion clinic.

If these two siblings had heard the message of sexual abstinence and of God's purity and holiness, this whole situation might have been avoided. If these children had been taught that sexuality is something beautiful, perhaps the story would have been different.

The process of childbirth is part of God's creative plan. He designed it with very concrete intentions. God designed the family to include one male and one female. All other relations that are outside of this design contradict the Word of God. On the sixth day of creation God created man and woman, in His image.

Answer the following questions.

List 5 main attributes of God that we should reflect.
1._____
2._____
3._____
4._____
5._____

What should our self-esteem be like since we were created in God's image?

_____

_____

_____

Which factors diminish the self-esteem of young people today?

_____

_____

_____

What is the relationship between a healthy self-esteem and remaining sexually abstinent until marriage?

_____

_____

In your opinion, what are the three main reasons for the high suicide rate among adolescents?

1._____

2._____

3._____

During the last 50 years the breakdown and decadence of the institution of marriage and the family has become quite evident. Approximately 4 out 10 married couples will end up divorced. Should that surprise us when couples arrive at the altar with divorce as an alternative or, as is readily practiced by the rich and affluent, with pre-nuptial agreements in anticipation of certain separation. Sexual relations are a gift from God designed by our Creator for our personal enjoyment, but reserved for the holy bond of matrimony.

Analyze the verses found in Genesis 2:20-25 and answer true or false to the following statements.

_____ 1. The church instituted marriage.

_____ 2. God created woman from the dust of the ground and breathed life into her.

_____ 3. God convinced Adam of his need for a suitable helper.

_____ 4. God did not create one sex superior to the other.

_____ 5. The woman was created from the flesh of Adam's side.

_____ 6. The marriage relationship substitutes but does not nullify the relationship of children with their parents.

_____ 7. The spiritual bond that is created as a result of the union between a man and his wife can only be broken by a divorce.

_____ 8. Once a man and a woman are united and become one flesh, the holy bond of matrimony is instituted.

_____ 9. Sexual relations outside of marriage negate the Word of God.

_____ 10. Bearing children outside of marriage violates one of God's divine principles.

Approximately 4 out 10 married couples will end up divorced. Should that surprise us when couples arrive at the altar with divorce as an alternative or, as it is readily practiced by the rich and affluent, with pre-nuptial agreements in anticipation of certain separation?

Write Genesis 2:24.

_____

_____

_____

_____

According to this verse, what are the 3 principles that originate the bond of matrimony?

_____

_____

_____

_____

Explain in your own words the principles we have studied which can be applied to Matthew 19:6.

_____

_____

_____

_____

List 5 reasons why children must be conceived within a marriage relationship.

1._____

2._____

3._____

4._____

5._____

The process of childbirth is a most gratifying experience for most women, because through her, God's promise is fulfilled. However, it continues to be an event filled with great intensity, mixed with strong emotions, intense pain and tremendous responsibility on the part of the medical personnel.

Women who are sterile (incapable of becoming pregnant) and who hope to conceive a child, often submit themselves to fertility treatments that generally are very expensive, and require persistence and patience. For a doctor, it's quite difficult to forget the sense of powerlessness and frustration in the face of such a patient, when another month goes by without the desired result.

Minerva Rivera was a patient with a medical history of infertility, but after receiving medication that induced and helped her ovulation, she became pregnant. Her age and the fact that this was her first child placed her in a high-risk category. At 40 weeks and 2 days of her gestation period, she visited our office and we decided to perform a C-section on her. She had been diagnosed with a benign tumor in the uterus, which made it impossible for her to give birth naturally, but contractions had already begun (Illustration 12).

Following a rigorous examination in which we checked her blood pressure, evaluated the presence or absence of proteins in the urine, and listened to the child's heartbeat, we found everything was stable and send her to the nearest hospital. Ninety minutes later I received an emergency call from the hospital. Our patient was experiencing a crisis. As I left the office I could not help wondering what went wrong — when she and her husband had gone to the hospital she was healthy and feeling quite happy.

When I arrived at the delivery room, I realized that the situation was extremely serious. There were at least 15 doctors present. The chief anesthesiologist informed me that my patient was dying. She was connected to an artificial breathing machine, and blood-filled foam spewed from her mouth. My legs buckled and a cold sweat ran down my face.

The Lord helped me to recover from my astonishment and consternation, and I managed to ask about the welfare of the baby. I quickly checked the heartbeat of the fetus and realized that the baby was also dying. I asked for a set of surgical instruments, and without moving the mother from the stretcher, performed a C-section. In only a few minutes we were able to deliver a baby girl in very poor physical condition, but alive.

Today, that little girl is 13 years old and enjoys perfect health; but unfortunately her mother died a few minutes after she was born. The autopsy report revealed that a massive embolism (obstruction caused by a clot in the veins of the lungs) from the amniotic fluid material was the cause of death. This is a very strange condition suffered by 1 out of 10,000 pregnant women.

God, in His divine plan of creation, planned for the human race to multiply through the union of a man and a woman. We can deduce that before the original sin committed by Adam and Eve, bringing children into the world

The process of childbirth is a most gratifying experience for a woman because it is in her, that God's promise is fulfilled. However, it does not cease to be an event filled with great intensity, mixed with strong emotions, intense pain and tremendous responsibility on the part of the medical personnel.

could have been a painless process without any medical complications or death. But after the fall, God in His sovereign decree punished man, and as a consequence, the whole human race.

Analyze Genesis 3:16 and explain what lesson can be learned.

_____

_____

_____

_____

_____

_____

_____

To the woman he said, "I will greatly increase your pains in childbearing; with pain you will give birth to children. Your desire will be for your husband, and he will rule over you."
—Genesis 3:16

The birth of a human being is a unique event, a creative miracle of God. We, His children, have been in the mind of God even before the foundation of the world, and as such should hold our very own lives in high esteem. We must recognize that all destructive thoughts that come into our lives are from Satan himself.

Write Ephesians 1:3-6.

_____

_____

_____

_____

Since when did God choose us?

_____

_____

What was God's purpose when He decided to redeem us?

_____

_____

_____

_____

God has a perfect plan for each of His children. We must dwell under the protection of the Word, and learn to wait on God's perfect timing.

God prepares the body of a woman for delivery. It is a process that — when free from any complications — is spontaneous and natural. This process requires a mature body and mind.

Read the verse found in Exodus 1:19 and answer the questions.

What was the order given to the Egyptian midwives?

_____

_____

_____

_____

What prompted such an order?

_____

_____

_____

A time to be born and a time to die, a time to plant and a time to uproot…a time to scatter stones and a time to gather them…a time to love and a time to hate.
—Ecclesiastes 3:2, 5, 8

When the midwives disobeyed Pharaoh's orders, which promise made to the Hebrew people was fulfilled?

_____

_____

_____

Prayer:

> *Heavenly Father, we thank you for the gift of life. We thank you because it is through your divine power that you have given us the ability to procreate. Teach us to treasure this privilege for your praise and glory, and teach us to use it in due time and for the right reasons. Amen.*

Lesson 4

Abortion and Its Consequences

Abortion is defined as the termination or loss of the product of conception, before it is deemed viable; which occurs around the 20th week of gestation. An abortion can be classified in two ways:

1- Spontaneous or natural: Due to a variety of medical conditions such as genetic, or acquired illnesses, trauma, accidents, biochemical disorders under which the mother's body rejects the fetus, poisoning, etc.

2- Induced or provoked: To preserve the life or the health of the mother, in case of rape or incest, to prevent the birth of a baby with abnormalities, or as a method of birth control.

An *incomplete abortion* occurs when only part of the product of conception is spontaneously expelled; and a *complete abortion* occurs when the entire product is expelled. The term *deferred abortion* refers to the period of time between the death of the product of conception and the expulsion of the content.

The *New Illustrated Dictionary of the Bible* tells us that as far back as the Old Testament laws, any person — man or woman — who would cause another person to abort would be punished, even by death. Even under the Assyrian laws, a system under which the law would only intervene in matters that pertained to the highest socio-economic levels of society, abortion was a punishable offence in which the individual was charged with a sizeable fine, whipped, forced to do hard labor, and even killed in the event that the fetus died. In other words, it was considered murder.

In the United States, it was not until 1973, following the now famous *Roe v. Wade* case, that abortion became legal. In this particular case, a woman who was raped by a gang took her case before the Supreme Court and demanded that she had a "right" to abort. The Supreme Court ruled in favor of her petition, and since then we have been responsible for the death of more than 30 million children. At present time we are confronted with the fateful statistic of 1.5 million abortions each year. More than thirty percent of these are performed on young people under the age of 18.

Murder is a crime that is condemned by the law of man and by the law of God.

The Giver of life, our Lord, is the only agent who has the authority to give life and to take it back. God has created life from the womb of the mother. The apostle Paul teaches in the Word of God that we were before the foundation of the world, which means that God knew us and had a purpose for us when we were still in our mother's womb. Furthermore, in His sovereignty, God bestowed upon us life and personality from the very moment He conceived us in His mind.

As Christians, it is our responsibility before God, and before men, to declare that abortion is a crime and nothing can justify it.

When we analyze the Scriptures, God's truths, as well as the promises he has in store for us, are revealed. We learn that from the time we were in our mother's womb he conferred upon us a holy calling. It's wonderful to know that God knows how He is going to use us and that our role is limited to discerning His will for our lives. The apostle Paul explained it to the Galatian church in the following way:

> When God, who set me apart from birth and called me by his grace…
> — Galatians 1:15

Throughout the Old and the New Testaments, the Word of God is clear. It asserts the reality of Creation for our lives. It was highly commendable the action taken by president George W. Bush, when only 48 hours after being sworn as president he vetoed a law that would have assigned millions of dollars to third world countries for the practice of abortions on demand. The prophet Isaiah experienced such a revelation of God's truth.

> Listen to me, you islands; hear this, you distant nations: Before I was born the LORD called me; from my birth He has made mention of my name.
> —Isaiah 49:1

> In a loud voice she exclaimed: "Blessed are you among women, and blessed is the child you will bear!"
> —Luke 1:42

See now that I myself am He! There is no god besides me. I put to death and I bring to life, I have wounded and I will heal, and no one can deliver out of my hand.
—Deuteronomy 32:29

You created my inmost being; you knit me together in my mother's womb…your eyes saw my unformed body. All the days ordained for me were written in your book before one of them came to be.
—Psalm 139:13,16

He chose us in him before the creation of the world to be holy and blameless in his sight.
—Ephesians 1:4

Scripture tells us the womb, and the fruit of the woman's womb is a gift from God. No one has the right to destroy it. God chose the womb of the woman to give shelter to the miracle of incarnation. Such a gift is a great privilege for women — when they allow God to use them in bringing to this world a fruit of life.

Did you know that every year more than 50,000 newborn children are sacrificed in satanic rituals throughout the United States? The same type of child sacrifices that occurred in ancient pagan cultic rituals in worship of the god Molech! We continue to bring a curse over our lives and allow the blood of the innocent to be spilled over our land. A nation that blatantly assaults the life of its children has reached the lowest level of perversion and moral degradation, vigorously denying the Word of God.

Abortion Techniques

A high school counselor invited us to speak to her students. She asked us to do her a favor and refrain from being too detailed when talking about abortion. In fact, she wanted us to totally eliminate the topic of abortion from our presentation. Her students had previously been taught that abortion is nothing more than another alternative in family planning.

But of course that's a concept with which we totally disagree. With great love and ethical concern we were able to convince the counselor that the students needed to expand their knowledge, and that if we didn't instruct them, they would go searching for answers somewhere else — and most likely, the ones they would find would be wrong. She finally agreed with our point of view — especially after seeing the positive reaction of the students as they were confronted with a reality they were not aware of.

The techniques used to practice an abortion have evolved over the past 40 years — from an injection of saline solution applied directly into the uterus of the pregnant woman, to the use of sophisticated chemical substances called *prostaglandins*. These medications resemble the substances that are naturally produced by the body to create the stretching and softening of the uterus and stimulate its contractions for delivery.

Lets examine the abortion techniques that are most commonly used:

1—Dilation and curettage: This is the procedure that is most often used during the first two months of pregnancy. It consists of expanding the diameter of the opening that serves as the entrance to the uterus. For this procedure an instrument that resembles a stiletto (a small dagger with a narrow, tapering blade) which varies in its thickness, is used. These instruments are called dilatadores. Once the desired expansion of the opening of the uterus has been obtained, an instrument that resembles a spoon with a hole in its center is introduced. This instrument has very sharp edges and is responsible for removing the life lodged inside the uterus.

2—Extraction by suction: This procedure is used in pregnancies that are more than two months old, and it is usually combined with the previous procedure. The uterus is dilated as previously explained, and a thick plastic hose is introduced into the uterine cavity. This hose is connected to a suction and negative pressure machine that tears the child away from the uterus and crushes him once it is turned on.

After 31/2 months, things become more complicated. By then the fetus is fully developed and has rapidly gained weight and size. Some 15 year ago, the stem of the Laminaria plant was used during this procedure because of its ability to dilate the uterus. The Laminaria plant has the shape of a cylinder of approximately 4 inches (10 centimeters). It produces chemicals which help soften the uterus and, when dilated, expel the products of conception. Today, doctors use substances that have a synthetic prostaglandin base that produce the same effect.

3—Abortion Pill RU 486: This has been recently approved for use by the Unites States Food and Drug Administration (FDA). The abortion pill RU 486, or Mifepristone has been used in Europe for many years. This drug is a substance, an artificial steroid, that blocks in the body of the patient the action of the hormone called progesterone, which is necessary in order to maintain the growth and development of the fertilized egg after conception. The pill can be taken up to 49 days after the time of conception to induce the abortion.

One of the negative psychological effects of RU 486 is that the fetus can be expelled from the body fully developed for his particular period of gestation. As a result, many women are impacted to the extent of experiencing great guilt when they see the fully-developed fetus — so much so that in some cases they

The first 49 days of conception represent the first seven weeks of a pregnancy, and by then the fetus has a heartbeat, its extremities are developed and its face has definition.

have performed full funeral and burial services for the baby. This is a great irony, isn't it. No mother in her right mind would kill her son and then have a funeral service in his honor.

The first 49 days of conception represent the first seven weeks of a pregnancy, and by then the fetus has a heartbeat, its extremities are developed and its face has definition.

Those who promote abortions rarely, if ever, talk about the physical, emotional and spiritual complications that are inherent to the practice of abortion. As a medical doctor who specializes in obstetrics and gynecology, I can provide faithful first-hand testimony of the huge number of complications that accompany this procedure: from severe hemorrhaging, infections, permanent sterility and loss of reproductive organs, perforation of the uterus or the intestines, and death. Also, there can be permanent illnesses, depression, psychosis, guilt, remorse, dementia, and suicide attempts.

On many occasions we've had to personally minister to women who, after 30 or 40 years, are still dealing with the memory of previous abortions. When we share with them that God is merciful and forgiving, they accept His forgiveness and become free from those terrible memories.

One of our most disturbing cases had to do with a 17-year-old girl named Norma who had done a pretty good job with guarding her purity and virginity. However, during her first year in college she did not have the ability to stand firm against the peer pressure from her friends, and she became pregnant by her boyfriend. The healthy relationship she kept with her family, a middle class educated family, allowed her to quickly confess her problem.

Her parents decided that the best solution to their ordeal was for her to have an abortion. They paid $300 for the procedure, totally unaware of the tragedy that was about to begin in their lives. A few days after the procedure, Norma developed a severe case of septicemia (a generalized internal infection) and suffered a cardiac arrest (her heart suddenly stopped beating). As a result, she had to be connected to an artificial breathing machine. She was transferred in very critical condition to the hospital where I practiced. After laboring intensely to save the girl's life, we took her to the operation theatre for emergency exploratory surgery (Illustration 15 and 16).

When a surgical incision was made in her abdomen, we discovered her abdominal cavity was filled with excrement due to a perforation in her intestine that resulted from the abortion procedure. Norma's life was saved, but she will not be able to have any children because all her reproductive organs had to be removed. Not only did she suffer a hysterectomy (removal of the uterus), but a colostomy procedure was also performed on her. A colostomy is an artificial anus that is made in the front part of the abdomen and is connected to a bag that collects the excrement. Today, Norma is a living testimony of the heavy price we could pay when we assault the life of a child.

How many other Normas are part of the unknown statistics? We'll probably never know, because their secrets are well guarded in expensive abortion clinics all over our country. How many others like her have lost their reproductive organs and will be forever scarred?

We must ask ourselves if it's worth it. Is it fair that young people are paying such a high price simply because, as a society we have been seduced and convinced that abortion is not a crime, just one of many alternatives? Freedom abused turns into licentiousness, to the extreme of staunchly denying the Word of God and its message of abstinence and sexual purity.

The Spirit of God has made me; the breath of the Almighty gives me life.
—Job 33:4

Recently, in Puerto Rico a doctor who performed abortions had his license revoked. Many of the young girls he treated nearly died. Finally, one woman who traveled from another country to have an abortion procedure done in his office did die.

It's painful to see how in this new millennium we are living in, an individual can take the life of another person under the excuse of family planning and do it in the freedom that the state bestows upon him to perform an abortion.

Read and write the following verses. What is the main idea in all of them?

1 Samuel 12:6

_____

_____

_____

_____

Job 12:10

_____

_____

_____

Job 33:4

_____

_____

_____

_____

God is the Author of life, and only He has power over it. In the Word of God certain situations are described where an abortion took place or a child was born dead due to indirect causes where the mother was not to blame.

Acts 17:25

_____

_____

_____

_____

Genesis 2:7

_____

_____

_____

_____

Psalm 119:73

_____

_____

_____

Isaiah 44:24

_____

_____

_____

God is the Author of life, and only He has power over it. In the Word of God certain situations are described when an abortion took place or a child was born dead due to indirect causes where the mother was not to blame.

In the following accounts, identify the cause of death of the fetus or child, due to accident, ill uterus, lack of mercy during a time of war, or the wickedness of evil and unjust men, and as God's judgment. Where it applies, explain how such a tragedy could have been avoided.

Exodus 21:22-23

_____

_____

_____

_____

2 Kings 8:12-13

_____

_____

_____

_____

Isaiah 13:16-19

_____

_____

_____

_____

God's property cannot be violated or destroyed by man. The life of all human beings, regardless of its chronological age, belongs to Him alone.

Hosea 9:14-16

_____

_____

_____

_____

Matthew 2:16-18

_____

_____

_____

_____

In the following verse there is a powerful biblical principle. If we understand it, having respect for other people's lives will be much easier. What is this principle?

Psalm 100:3

_____

_____

_____

_____

God's property cannot be violated or destroyed by man. The life of all human beings, regardless of their chronological age, belongs to Him alone. It's shameful to realize how little we value our lives, especially the life of the unborn. How does God see our children? Explain the following verses.

Isaiah 29:23

_____

_____

_____

_____

Psalm 127:3

_____

_____

_____

_____

Read Isaiah 43:7. Why, and for what reason, does God give us life?

_____

_____

_____

_____

What consequences will those who practice abortions face? Write the following verses and in your own words explain what they say.

Matthew 5:21

_____

_____

_____

_____

Hebrews 10:30-31

_____

_____

_____

_____

2 Peter 2:9

_____

_____

_____

_____

God has not been silent on the subject of abortion. We have been able to prove that through the verses previously mentioned. The Word of God is clear: the fetus is a person. That means abortion is a crime because it destroys the life of a person not yet born.

Answer the following questions:

Who gave us life?

_____

_____

Since when does the Lord have knowledge of who we are?

_____

_____

According to the central idea of the verse, who is the only one with absolute authority over our lives?

_____

_____

Besides a personal knowledge, what other blessing did God bestow upon the prophet when he was still in his mother's womb?

_____

_____

_____

Bring my sons from afar and my daughters from the ends of the earth — everyone who is called by my name, whom I created for my glory, whom I formed and made.
—Isaiah 43:6-7

Jesus was recognized while still in his mother's womb; his cousin John had the same experience. Write the verse found in Luke 1:15 and then explain what blessings were promised to John the Baptist and when they were to begin.

_____

_____

_____

_____

Many times people allege they don't know that abortion is a crime, or they defend their actions by rationalizing that abortion has been legalized. There are many legalized issues, such as smoking or drinking alcoholic beverages by people over 21 years of age, which are not a crime in most states. But the fact that something has been legalized, and therefore not penalized by the law, does not mean that it is right. In fact, it may very well be totally wrong when confronted by the authoritative Word of God.

Read Proverbs 24:11-12 and answer True (T) or False (F) to the following statements:

_____ We should not help those who are heading for a certain death.

_____ We must save those who are in danger of dying.

_____ Abortion presupposes a danger to the unborn child.

_____ Such crime is punished by the Word of God.

_____ Because it has been legalized, abortion is not a crime as far as God is concerned.

_____ God knows and searches our real intentions.

_____ We will only receive rewards for our good works, not retribution for our bad works.

_____ If we sincerely repent after participating in an abortion procedure, God will forgive us.

Answer the following questions:

What are the three main truths implicit in Proverbs 24:11-12?

1._____

2._____

3._____

Many times people allege not knowing that abortion is a crime, or defend their actions by rationalizing that abortion has been legalized.

From what type of death did Jesus rescue us?

_____

What is the difference between remorse and repentance? Explain.

_____

_____

_____

_____

Different statistical studies have found that a certain degree of violence is generated against children who are fatherless, children whose parents have remarried and even against the unborn.

Answer the following questions based on Proverbs 24:11-12.

What is the "inheritance" that belongs to the unborn child?

_____

_____

_____

What are the rights of the unborn?

_____

_____

Who guarantees such rights?

_____

_____

_____

What alternative would you present to an unwed 16-year-old who wishes to abort?

_____

_____

_____

Usually, the court is the institution in charge of assigning a jury or a judge to decide upon, and apply, the death penalty to a prisoner. On many occasions

The word of the LORD came to me, saying, "Before I formed you in the womb I knew you, before you were born I set you apart; I appointed you as a prophet to the nations."
—Jeremiah 1:4-5

these prisoners wait many years on death row while they appeal their conviction. Yet the baby that is about to be aborted doesn't have anyone who will defend his case and his right to live, and oftentimes such a decision rests upon the shoulders of people who do not love or want him.

As you consider the next few verses, explain in your own words what God says to us when we spill innocent blood.

Revelation 22:15

_____

_____

_____

_____

Revelation 21:8

_____

_____

_____

_____

Romans 1:18

_____

_____

_____

_____

Romans 1:29-31

_____

_____

_____

_____

Genesis 9:6

_____

_____

_____

_____

Proverbs 6:16-17

_____

_____

_____

_____

Now that you have finished this lesson and completed the assigned exercises, answer the following questions in your own words and use a verse from Scripture to prove your argument.

What is the definition of abortion?

_____

_____

_____

_____

_____

What would be your main argument as you debate against the practice of abortion?

_____

_____

_____

_____

Why does the practice of abortion represent a risk to the physical and spiritual well being of the individual?

_____

_____

_____

_____

How does having been created in God's image refute the practice of abortion?

_____

_____

_____

_____

_____

List three possible medical complications that can result from an abortion.

1._____

2._____

3._____

Whoever sheds the blood of man, by man shall his blood be shed; for in the image of God has God made man.
—Genesis 9:6

Prayer:

Heavenly Father, we ask that you give us the wisdom of your Word in order to live in times as difficult as these. We pray for each young girl or woman who is in the process of deciding if they should have an abortion, or not. We ask that you enlighten their understanding and show them how this action violates the laws of creation that you established. Forgive us for all the killings of babies that have been committed and for the ones that continue to die. Be merciful with us. Amen.

Whoever sheds the blood of man, by man shall his blood be shed; for in the image of God has God made man.
—-Genesis 9:6

Lesson 5

A Dating Relationship Approved by God

God created us with feelings and emotions, with the ability to love, and the need for affection. He is the Creator of every cell, organ and system in our body, and, in His omniscience knows precisely what we need.

This is why it's important for us to discern God's will for our lives. In this case, specifically about when it is the right moment and who the person is that God has reserved for us to establish a serious dating relationship with — one that will lead to a future marriage.

A dating relationship that is approved by God is one that has been planned by Him, without the intervention of our human desires and expectations. When we allow God to reign sovereign over our lives, these truths will become a reality, and will allow the relationship to flow spontaneously, and above all, under God's blessing. These principles stand totally against the thought and trend of this world — that relationships lack seriousness and commitment.

A dating relationship that is approved by God is a supernatural process, the beginning of a course that should lead us to the altar. Throughout this study we have established what the bond of matrimony represents before God. Using this same type of reasoning we can also see the importance of a dating relationship approved by God.

Legalism and senseless reasoning just obstruct the channels of communication between people. Concepts rooted in human wisdom are dangerous and simply do not work. The truth found in the Word is more than sufficient in itself. Nothing should be added to it. The Word of God is changeless. If God says something should be holy, then it must be sanctified. The dating relationship is part of God's master plan for humanity, but only and exclusively within the boundaries He has established.

It was the third time in a single month that this mother had visited our office with her 17-year-old daughter. We had referred her to a colleague, a skin specialist, because the young lady had developed strange and worrisome spots

Can a man scoop fire into his lap without his clothes being burned? Can a man walk on hot coals without his feet being scorched?
—Proverbs 6:27-28

Even the very hairs of your head are all numbered.
—Matthew 10:30

on her back and legs. I was impatient to read the skin biopsy report and hoped that the lesions on her body were not the result of AIDS or an infection caused by a sexually transmitted disease.

Both her mother and I were greatly relieved when the report showed that that this young woman had a simple skin inflammation, caused on many occasions by nerves, tension or stress.

Though she was still a virgin, each relationship had stolen a piece of her heart.

When I asked the mother about her daughter's personal life she was silent, and asked the daughter to wait outside of the office. Then the mother began to cry uncontrollably as she told us about her daughter's state of severe depression. She told us that her daughter accused her of a lack of counsel and discipline, because her mother had allowed her to have her first boyfriend at the age of 13, and many others after that. Even though most were from the church they attended, the 17-year-old girl felt used, rejected, and singled out as "easy." Though she was still a virgin, each relationship had stolen a piece of her heart. At such an early age she already had deep scars in the innermost parts of her being.

As her mother cried in desperation, she admitted her mistake. She recognized that what she had considered something innocent and normal for the times in which we live, had seriously damaged her daughter.

Be self-controlled and alert. Your enemy the devil prowls around like a roaring lion looking for someone to devour.
—1 Peter 5:8

As we previously learned, the soul is the seat of the emotions, memories and afflictions. And since we are integral beings, the soul has the ability to manifest itself in the body. The numerous lesions all over this young woman's skin were the result of a psychosomatic state of anemia (lack of vitality or courage). In other words, her illness had been caused by mental factors. Her body had become a faithful witness to the brokenness, lack of joy and low self-esteem that had taken place in her spirit. And to this, add the guilt complex imposed on her by the enemy of our souls.

The scars caused by this type of experience can manifest themselves years later in the form of a dysfunctional marriage relationship affected by unresolved memories, or situations that were never surrendered to the Lord.

We are all exposed to the rules that this world dictates. When secular humanism knocks at our doors, we Christians frequently give in to the offers of the world.

So-called sex experts tell couples to know each other sexually first, in order to find out if they are sexually compatible before marriage. The movie industry and the mass media tell us premarital sex is normal, desirable, expected.

A good analogy could be smoking. The tobacco industry in the United States has had to pay out a great many millions of dollars as a direct result of an avalanche of civil lawsuits from almost every state in the nation. The relationship between tobacco and death from lung cancer has been proven a fact, and after many legal battles, the industry responsible for a devastating health problem has been penalized.

In the same manner, why not hold the "sex industry," in all its manifestations, as accountable as the tobacco industry? This industry is equally harmful to the health of an entire nation. It assaults a whole generation of young people and it sins against God.

Following a time of sharing with a group of young people in a church, a young man, holding an 8-month-old baby in his arms, called us aside. Although he had recently celebrated his 17th birthday, He appeared to be much older.

He told us his parents, leaders in another church, had recommended that he marry, at the age of 16, a girl he had known for only eight months. We asked if the reason for the marriage was pregnancy, or because they had been sexually active. To our surprise, the young man said that the only reason his parents had for wanting them to get married was to avoid seeing the two of them give into pre-marital sex.

Now, he said, they were experiencing many difficulties in their marriage. He said he didn't feel fulfilled as a man, and that he didn't think he really knew his wife.

In trying to avoid a possible problem, the young man's parents had created an even more serious one. They tried to help God; and in the process they assumed an erroneous role, one in which they violated many principles concerning a dating relationship and marriage.

No one should enter into a marriage relationship out of convenience. It should be a mutual agreement between two mature and responsible individuals who

No one should enter into a marriage relationship out of convenience. It should be a mutual agreement between two mature and responsible individuals who understand that they are meant for each other and have God at the center of their relationship.

understand that they are meant for each other and have God at the center of their relationship.

During my second year of medical residency in obstetrics and gynecology, I received an urgent call from the hospital's radiology department. When I arrived, I was greatly surprised when I was asked to assist in delivering the baby of a 17-year-old girl in this non-sterile environment.

The desperate parents had brought their daughter to the hospital because she was suffering strong abdominal pains, and had a previous history of kidney stones. The doctor who was in charge of the emergency room, half-asleep, believed the parents' assessment of the situation and without examining the patient first, sent her to have X-rays taken. While in the radiology department, the girl gave birth prematurely at 7 1/2-months.

Although this event took place almost 22 years ago, I can still remember the parents' expressions of anguish, desperation, and shock.

As a father and doctor I've heard many stories of dating relationships in different parts of the world. Hearing these testimonies confirms in my mind that without a doubt, we have forgotten and altered the concept of a dating relationship approved by God.

The time to begin a serious dating relationship is when God has revealed the person that you are to marry. When you allow God to be at the center of the issue, you can be certain that your choice will be the correct one. When this happens, no obstacle can prevent that which God has determined. You can then begin a dating relationship with a God-centered foundation.

This concept may sound radical and absolute, but it is biblical. In today's society absolute concepts have lost their charm and are criticized because they are thought to stand against the individual's freedom and sense of individuality. But our God is not a democratic God. He is not led by a consensus of public opinion; He is theocratic, and His Word is absolute and unchangeable. It's up to us whether to accept His counsel, or disobey and ignore Him. Realize this, though: When we disobey, we will suffer great consequences.

The obedience and purity that God demands from us continues to be a truth that is absolute and unchangeable. It is non-negotiable; it stands against the lies of the world.

The obedience and purity that God demands from us continues to be a truth that is absolute and unchangeable. It is non-negotiable; it stands against the lies of the world. God humiliates those who think they are wise in their own opinions and refuse to value His Word. They eventually are trapped by their own webs of ignorance and disobedience.

The secret to success in life is being at peace with God, and being able to discern God's moment and the moment to make the correct decision.

We issue you a challenge: Consider the intensity with which you seek God's wisdom concerning your choice of a career, the ministry where you should serve, and so many other things. Be even more intense in requesting God's help in discerning the appropriate time, moment, and person that He has prepared for you. The dating relationship that is approved by God is a serious commitment that should prepare you to share with and to know the person that God has prepared and destined to be your mate before the foundation of the world.

Why would a couple of 13 and 14-year olds begin a dating? Statistics have proven that the younger a girl is when she has a boyfriend, the higher the possibility that she will lose her virginity before the age of 17. Ninety-one percent of girls that begin to date at the age of 12 are sexually active before the age of 17.

Premature relationships with someone other than the person who will one day be your marriage partner are, in most cases, a dead-end street. They have no genuine purpose other than momentary personal enjoyment and satisfying selfish desires. The end product of such a relationship is usually a sense of frustration, bitterness and deep emotional scars.

Intimate physical relations, imprudent fondling and illicit sexual relations during dating limit your capacity to give and to receive love in marriage. It pleased God to decree that your desires and sexual appetites are to be consummated only within the bond of matrimony. The violation of these divine principles will hurt you emotionally and spiritually, provoking within you feelings of guilt, shame and undesired memories that will eventually affect your marriage relationship.

Statistics have proven that the younger a girl is when she has a boyfriend, the higher the possibility that she will lose her virginity before the age of 17.

Premature and out-of-season relationships with someone other than the person that will one day be your marriage partner are, in most cases, a dead-end street. There is no genuine purpose other than momentary personal enjoyment and satisfying selfish desires. The end product of such a relationship is usually a sense of frustration, bitterness and deep emotional scars.

Sexual abstinence and a dating relationship approved by God, is not an abstract or unreal concept that is impossible to live out. Neither is it one more method of family planning, or a new rule of Christian conduct. It's what God wants and demands from us. He has ordered that we refrain from surrendering to the appetites and passions of our flesh. That which the world accepts and promotes is an abomination before God. Sexual abstinence is a lifestyle. With God's help, we can deny ourselves and refuse to give in to the desires of the flesh.

Let's search the Scriptures.

It's almost impossible to reach a consensus concerning freedoms and prohibitions during a dating relationship; therefore, the wise and intelligent thing to do is search the authoritative Book on the subject — the Word of God. Paul had the gift of celibacy, but he was also very much aware of the temptations faced by single people.

Write the following verses and answer the questions:

1 Corinthians 7:7-9

_____

_____

What advice does Paul give to those who cannot live a life of abstinence?

_____

_____

1 Corinthians 10:23

_____

_____

_____

What actions are not permissible in a dating relationship?

_____

_____

1 Peter 2:11

_____

_____

What is Paul's warning to us?

_____

_____

_____

Galatians 5:24

_____

_____

_____

The Word says that God has given us self-control and that we must use it every moment in order to preserve our lives and obey God.

Christian dating relationships must use the Word of God as a guide. What is Paul's reminder in 1 Corinthians 10:13?

_____

_____

Those who belong to Christ Jesus have crucified the sinful nature with its passions and desires.
—Galatians 5:24

Is it possible to live a life of sexual abstinence? Why?

_____

_____

_____

The Word says that God has given us self-control and that at every moment we must use it in order to preserve our lives and obey God. Explain the relationship between these verses and sexual abstinence.

Proverb 25:28

_____

_____

_____

Proverbs 6:27-28

_____

_____

_____

Proverb 13:14

_____

_____

_____

One of the most common questions asked of us in all of our presentations is how far a dating couple can go in their physical intimacy. Our answer is always the same. A couple that wishes to please God with their behavior must recognize we carry our sinful nature with us everywhere. Although we are saved and recognize that the blood of Jesus has cleansed us, we continue to live in this world and walk around with a sinful body that responds and yields to the appetites of the flesh.

No single person who is clear about this truth, must tempt, test or flirt with temptation. We must never attempt to prove that we are stronger than sin; such a challenge is not in our best interest.

Analyze these verses about Joseph and answer the following questions:

> *Though she spoke to Joseph day after day, he refused to go to bed with her or even be with her. One day he went into the house to attend to his duties, and none of the household servants was inside. She caught him by the cloak and said, "Come to bed with me!" But he left his cloak in her hand and ran out of the house.*
> —*Genesis 39:10-12*

How did Joseph earn the trust of his master Potiphar?

_____
_____
_____

What was the main reason Joseph refused the continual sexual invitations from Potiphar's wife?

_____
_____
_____

What was Joseph's immediate reaction when Potiphar's wife caught him by his cloak?

_____
_____
_____

Why did Joseph decide to run instead of trying to convince Potiphar's wife to give him back his cloak?

_____

_____

_____

When a dating relationship is guided by the fear of the Lord, there are no doubts as to the rules of conduct we must follow. Under no circumstance will we expose ourselves to out-of-the-way places, trips alone as a couple, intimate physical contact, passionate kisses, or caressing each other's erogenous zones, all of which lead to heightened sexual arousal and, ultimately, intercourse. We must say no to everything that goes against the holiness and purity that God demands from us. Only God, His Word and a commitment to sexual abstinence will help us to keep the carnal desires and dishonest passions in check.

What does the Bible recommend in Hebrews 13:4?

_____

_____

_____

God desires a dating/courtship relationship that is pure. This purity and obedience before God will help us to be husbands and wives that are emotionally and physically healthy and stable.

What does 1 Thessalonians 4:1-7 say about the will of God concerning our sexuality?

_____

_____

_____

According to Ephesians 5:3-7, God clearly despises which things?

_____

_____

_____

Read Proverbs 30:18-19 and list those things that are prohibited.

_____

_____

_____

According to 1 Corinthians 6:18-20 why are sins against the body so grave in God's sight?

_____

_____

_____

The Word of God refers to the church as the bride of the Lamb when it speaks of Christ's return and the wedding between the two. Symbolically, it speaks to us about the bride's attitude as she anxiously waits for her wedding day.

Why will the bride be dressed in fine linen? Revelation 19:7-8.

_____

_____

_____

When a dating relationship is guided by the fear of the Lord, there are no doubts as to the rules of conduct we must follow....We must say no to everything that goes against the holiness and purity that God demands from us.

According to 2 Corinthians 11:2-3, what is the danger of not exercising good judgment?

_____

_____

_____

_____

List those sins that cloud our judgment.

_____

_____

_____

What is the only alternative for being victorious over such sins?

_____

_____

_____

_____

According to Ephesians 5:25-27, what is the similarity between the bride of the Lamb and a girl involved in a Christian dating relationship?

_____

_____

_____

What is the similarity between the groom in the wedding of the Lamb and a young man involved in a Christian dating relationship?

_____

_____

_____

What are the characteristics of love as described in 1 Corinthians 13:4-7?

_____

_____

_____

What is the difference between physical attraction and love as described in 1 Corinthians 1:5-7?

_____

_____

_____

I am jealous for you with a godly jealousy. I promised you to one husband, to Christ, so that I might present you as a pure virgin to him. But I am afraid that just as Eve was deceived by the serpent's cunning, your minds may somehow be led astray from your sincere and pure devotion to Christ.
—2 Corinthians 11:2-3

Read Ecclesiastes 11:9-10. What is the main message?

_____

_____

_____

What relationship exists between the flesh, wickedness and adolescence?

_____

_____

_____

What was Solomon's grave mistake as described in Ecclesiastes 2:10-11?

_____

_____

_____

_____

What is the advice given in Proverbs 3:21-26?

_____

_____

_____

_____

What is our reward if we obey the Word of God?

_____

_____

_____

_____

The Word of God is clear and effective. We must be careful not to act according to our own understanding, falling prey to Satan's lies.

Do not be misled: "Bad company corrupts good character."
—1 Corinthians 15:33

Read and write the verse found in Isaiah 5:20.

_____

_____

_____

_____

In your own words, summarize the central message of the verse.

_____

_____

_____

_____

Prayer:

> *Heavenly Father, we thank you for Your holy Word. Thank you because it is through your Word that we can know Your will. We ask that You help us live under the guidance of Your commandments and teachings, that we may live a life that is pure and pleasing in Your sight. Help us enjoy a dating relationship that is approved by You, and to remain pure until the day we marry. Amen.*

Lesson 6

Peer Pressure

We were in the process of celebrating the third meeting of the men's ministry at Glenview Baptist Church, in the city of Ponce, Puerto Rico. An enthusiastic group had gathered and listened attentively as we shared about the role of the man as priest of his home and the need to recognize the many ways in which our children are affected by peer pressure.

To illustrate the dangers of peer pressure a dramatized sequence of events was presented in which a group of young people challenged one of their peers to prove how truly brave he was by participating in a drag race against someone else.

The chosen dramatization was based on a real life situation in which five young people lost their lives. Following the first part of the drama the group was shown a video in which both young men were sitting in their cars prior to the race. Then the race was dramatized from the start to the resulting fatal accident. After the video presentation, the actor who played one of the dead young men shared all the details related to the accident and "his" own death.

Once the presentation was over, we continued with the conference, but noticed that one of the men from the audience was approaching the podium. He was crying and deeply burdened. His steps were heavy and slow as if he were carrying a great load. We all empathized with this man's pain, and wondered what was wrong. Once the man was able to calm down, he approached the microphone and spoke these words to the group:

"Today is the 6th anniversary of my son's death. He was killed in a car accident along with four friends. They were driving a car that is similar to the one we saw in the video. Because of peer pressure, he found himself in the wrong place at the wrong time. I personally had to drag my son out that car. I bitterly remember his open, unseeing eyes and his demolished body. You can't imagine how painful it is to lose a child in such a tragic manner."

For you created my inmost being, you knit me together in my mother's womb. I praise you because I am fearfully and wonderfully made; your works are wonderful, I know that full well. My frame was not hidden from you when I was made in the secret place. When I was woven together in the depths of the earth.
—Psalm 139:13-15

I immediately put my notes away. There was nothing written there that could add anything to the reality of peer pressure and its effects. We dedicated the rest of the time to praying for this brother and to intercede and cry out loud for the safety of our own sons and daughters. That tragic "coincidence" (although we know that with God there is no such thing as a coincidence) left and indelible mark on that group of men.

Peer pressure is defined as a force or attraction that a particular group, or even an individual, exercises over another person, causing them to participate in acts that otherwise they would not. The affected person renounces all personal values and principles and agrees to do whatever the group is doing and to imitate their behavior. On many occasions, the things that are done directly challenge the counsel of God's Word.

It is because of peer pressure that young people take their initial steps into the world of drugs, alcohol, pornography, foul language, perverse music, rebellion, delinquency, and even sexual relationships outside of marriage. What motivates young people to give in to peer pressure? The answer to this question is varied and could take many books to fully explain.

What we must understand is that peer pressure has always existed and will always exist. It's your responsibility to learn to face such pressure in the different and varied situations of your life. It's essential to understand that you can be victorious over peer pressure, but it will cost you something.

Not too long ago, the island of Puerto Rico was shaken to its core by a tragic event. A 15-year-old girl who had been arguing with her mother took a towel, and in a premeditated move wrapped it around her mother's head and shot her in the back of the neck. The event resembled the script for a horror movie.

Following an exhaustive investigation, it was shown that the girl's personality began to change after she met a group of young people that dressed in black and promoted satanic rituals and all kinds of violence against parents and authority figures.

In her last court appearance, the girl was found to be mentally competent. She will be tried as an adult. Because there is no death penalty in Puerto Rico, she will most likely face a sentence of life in prison. She went from being an easy-going young lady with excellent grades, to a murderer, all because of peer pressure.

Unfortunately, over the past several years, this type of crime has become more common all across the United States.

Why are these groups so attractive? What makes peer pressure so powerful? Why are young people willing to set aside their values and ideals without stopping to consider the high price they must pay? What motivates them to risk losing their very own lives just to belong to a particular group? Why does the love and respect they feel for their parents and others suddenly occupy a second place in their lives?

In studying the literature that relates to this phenomenon it seems as if all the experts think they have the right answers to these problems. But we must be honest with ourselves and recognize that theirs are not valid answers when we consider the large numbers of young people that are destroying their own lives and the lives of others — many times by way of suicide. Having been raised in dysfunctional homes is a factor that greatly affects a young persons' decision-making process.

Though my father and mother forsake me, the LORD will receive me.
—Psalm 27:10

Let's look at some of the reasons that can lead a young person into yielding to peer pressure:

    Low self esteem

    The absence of an authority figure

    Lack of effectiveness

    Lack of acceptance by a previous group

    Absence of moral values

    Mass media contamination

    Poor role of government and church leadership: corruption and bad examples

    Increasing violence — at school and home

    Child and adolescent abuse

    Unresolved emotional conflicts, chronic depression, phobias, confused behavior patterns, inferiority complex, etc.

A father to the fatherless, a defender of widows, is God in his holy dwelling.
—Psalm 68:5

Many of these reasons and emotional conflicts are quite serious. It's difficult having to admit that the origin for most of these problems is the absence of God in the family unit. But the hard fact is, many of these problems begin when we ignore the Word of God and focus, instead, on pleasing ourselves or someone else.

The Word of God is the fountain of all wisdom.

In today's world, young people are exposed to unbelievable pressures, and are exposed to a society that is declining morally and spiritually, where those who call themselves "experts" teach that the Word of God has become obsolete and that sexual abstinence is nothing more than a fantasy. They've left us with very few alternatives and elements of judgment that can be used in making correct decisions. As a result, young people have lost any ability to discern between what is good and bad, real or fake, holy and impure.

But all is not lost. God continues to be in control. The Word of God continues to be the answer, and sexual abstinence, purity and holiness, are the alternatives. God mocks the wisdom of man. At the end of the road, we must, and will, recognize that the Word of God is the only truth there is.

Let's search the Scriptures about this subject:

The goal of peer pressure is to persuade one person or many people to follow or execute another's desires and plan, and to adopt another's ideas, although they themselves might harbor some doubts. On many occasions, this type of pressure has satanic roots. In Jesus' times this was precisely the strategy used by Satan to destroy and bring shame upon the gospel. Peer pressure was part of the plan used to persuade the people to crucify the Lord.

Analyze Matthew 27:20-26. Who persuaded or used peer pressure with the people that led to the crucifixion of Christ? How did they do it?

_____

_____

_____

_____

_____

We can see that even after the death of Jesus, the same groups continued to exercise pressure in order force things to be done according to their perverse set of ideas.

Read the following verses and write the intentions of the pressure groups:
Matthew 28:11-15

_____

_____

_____

Luke 20:1-8

_____

_____

_____

Acts 14:19-20

_____

_____

_____

The Word of God warns against this terrible act of seduction by the enemy. We must know the Scriptures so as to avoid being deceived and manipulated with lies or with half-truths.

What advice does Paul give to young Timothy and to the Colossian church?

2 Timothy 3:10-16

_____

_____

_____

According to Paul, what will happen to those who are deceivers of men? What must we do to protect ourselves form them?

_____

_____

_____

_____

Colossians 2:1-4

_____

_____

_____

Some Jews came from Antioch and Iconium and won the crowd over. They stoned Paul and dragged him outside the city, thinking he was dead.
—Acts 14:19

The strategy of these pressure groups favors sexual licentiousness, as well as vain, shallow arguments against abstinence, arguments without a solid foundation. If we were to ask these people about the content of their arguments concerning sexual abstinence, they would only argue that it takes away their freedom to enjoy life. Whatever other ideas they express are far from the truth, and are fatally mistaken.

Sexual abstinence is precisely the only way to live a life of freedom, to make wise decisions, and to cease being slaves bound by our passions and carnal desires. The saddest thing of all is that those who surrender to peer pressure become slaves of other slaves — and the master of both is Satan himself.

Read and meditate upon the following verses:

2 Peter 2:18-19

Jesus replied: "I tell you the truth, everyone who sins is a slave to sin."
—John 8:34

_____

_____

_____

John 8:34

_____

_____

_____

Are you are being influenced by peer pressure? Do you realize that you are participating in behavior that is not right, and want to put and end to it? Does your weakness make it difficult to break with such behavior? Allow me to share an extraordinary word of encouragement with you: **God can help you to be free**. All you have to do is recognize that you have sinned, truly repent, and ask God to help you pay the price of living in complete sexual abstinence. I assure you that He will help you. God does not want us to be slaves to sin, much less allow someone else to drag us into a life of sin.

Is it possible for you to live a life of sexual abstinence? Explain your answer.

_____

_____

_____

_____

Write the next verses and read each one out loud.

Matthew 19:26

_____

_____

_____

Luke 18:27

_____

_____

_____

In the Old Testament there are examples of young people who were able to conquer peer pressure. As a result, God honored their faithfulness. Read the following verses and in your own words describe the events mentioned.

Daniel 6:1-28

_____

_____

_____

What and who helped Daniel conquer peer pressure?

_____

_____

_____

What effect did Daniel's determination to please God rather than man, have on the lives of those who were observing him?

_____

_____

_____

Did Daniel doubt at any moment that God would strengthen him during such a difficult time in his life?

_____

_____

_____

_____

Now when Daniel learned that the decree had been published, he went home to his upstairs room where the windows opened toward Jerusalem. Three times a day he got down on his knees and prayed, giving thanks to his God just as he had done before.
—_Daniel 6:10_

How can we use the Word of God to become free from peer pressure? Read the following verses and write them down.

John 8:31-36

_____

_____

_____

2 Corinthians 3:16-18

_____

_____

_____

Galatians 5:1

_____

_____

_____

Young Daniel resolved in his heart to please God instead of men. Write Daniel 6:10-11 and meditate upon the verses:

_____

_____

_____

It is for freedom that Christ has set us free. Stand firm, then, and do not let yourselves be burdened again by a yoke of slavery.
—Galatians 5:1

Daniel received the strength he needed to walk in righteousness. Do you think that today there are many young people like Daniel? Explain

_____

_____

_____

In the Old Testament book of Genesis, we find another courageous young man. His name is Joseph, one of Jacob's sons. We have read a little about him already. Now read Genesis chapter 39 and write verses 8 and 9.

_____

_____

_____

_____

_____

Who or whom did Joseph want not to offend with his behavior?

_____

_____

_____

What did the wife of Joseph's master wish to provoke in him?

_____

_____

_____

Why did Joseph run from the house and not stay and try to persuade the woman of her wrong and seductive behavior?

_____

_____

_____

_____

> *Flee the evil desires of youth, and pursue righteousness, faith, love and*
> *peace, along with those who call on the Lord out of a pure heart.*
> *—2 Timothy 2:22*

What is the similarity with this passage and the story of Joseph? To whom is this passage directed?

_____

_____

_____

_____

Was Joseph's punishment just? Why?

_____

_____

_____

_____

On many occasions we may find ourselves in situations where man's justice will fail, and the only thing that will sustain us is God's faithfulness and His Word. Read the following verses. Write what they tell you about how God works in our lives.

Genesis 39:2-3

_____

_____

_____

Analyze and explain the following verses in your own words:
Ecclesiastes 7:26

_____

_____

_____

Seduction is one of the many masks used by groups that exercise pressure over us. This could be a terrible bondage; and as such it is better to run than to give in to it.

Proverbs 5:3-5

_____

_____

_____

_____

Romans 8:8

_____

_____

_____

Write the following verse and mention the particular things or situations that control you or cause you to feel pressure.

1 Corinthians 6:12

_____

_____

_____

The apostle Paul makes this declaration to the believers in Corinth because they had been seduced and pressured into illicit sexual practices. Young people who have experienced freedom when they decide to obey the Word of God have experienced the joy of true freedom from unchecked sexual appetites.

On many occasions we may find ourselves in situations where man's justice will fail, and the only thing that will sustain us is God's faithfulness and His Word.

Seduction is one of the many lures used by groups that exercise pressure over us. This could be a terrible bondage; and as such it is better to run than to give in to it.

Young Rehoboam, the son and successor to King Solomon, became a victim of peer pressure. Read I Kings 12:1-24.

To whom did Rehoboam go for counsel?

_____

_____

_____

_____

Why did he choose to listen to the advice of the young men?

_____

_____

_____

_____

Was this a good decision? Explain.

_____

_____

_____

In the Old Testament we find the story of Tamar, the daughter of King David that was raped. The most surprising thing about this event is that she was raped by her half brother, Amnon. Read and analyze the account that appears in 2 Samuel 13:1-39.

Who advised Amnon and pressured him into committing such a crime?

_____

_____

_____

_____

What was young Tamar's reaction?

_____

_____

_____

_____

_____

He followed the advice of the young men and said, "My father made your yoke heavy; I will make it even heavier. My father scourged you with whips; I will scourge you with scorpions."
—I Kings 12:14

Read the verses found in 2 Samuel 13:14-19. What were the consequences of such a regrettable event?

_____

_____

_____

How was Tamar's rape avenged? What was the reaction of her father, King David?

_____

_____

_____

_____

Amnon had a friend named Jonadab son of Shimeah, David's brother. Jonadab was a very shrewd man... ."Go to bed and pretend to be ill," Jonadab said. "When your father comes to see you, say to him, 'I would like my sister Tamar to come and give me something to eat.'"

—2 Samuel 13:3, 5

Prayer:

Heavenly Father, we come before you recognizing that you are our fortress and will help us to resist the pressures that come from Satan and from the world around us. Your Word is our truth and shield. We declare that You have not given us a spirit of fear but of power and self-control. Amen.

Lesson 7

Sexual Problems and Deviations

A certain city in the United States characterized by liberal attitudes that border on licentiousness, and where the largest number of AIDS patients can be found, has been the scene of numerous sexual scandals. A celebration by the Pedophile Association took place under the authority of the city's mayor. Under the escort and protection of the city's police force, the participants paraded through the streets of the city carrying posters and banners demanding that they be allowed to exercise their right to participate in all types of sexual relations with children.

Pedophilia is recognized as a psychological-sexual disorder through which an adult is sexually stimulated and gratified as a result of contact with pre-adolescent children. The typical pedophile is not able to obtain sexual satisfaction in a relationship with another adult. They normally suffer from low self-esteem and understand that a relationship with a child is much less complicated and easier to control. The child that has been victimized may on occasion develop sexual problems as an adult, and may even become a sexual victimizer himself. When a young girl is abused this way, her reaction is usually self-destructive, and with time may erode into a lifestyle of prostitution and drug abuse.

A few weeks after the authorized parade, the police received confidential information that something weird was about to take place in an exclusive pedophile club in the city. After obtaining a search warrant, the authorities raided the club and were witnesses to a gruesome scene: A group of men was watching, via closed-circuit television, the violation of a young child by an adult male.

Human life is a divine gift, designed, created, and sustained by God. As an integral part of this life, God instituted the family and would consolidate it through the holy bond of matrimony. This has been established by God, is a basic principle in His Word, and even though secular humanism and all who defend deviant sexual practices refuse to accept it, marriage continues to be a valid principle. God designed the body of the woman and the man so that they can come together in a physical union, and become one flesh.

Because of this, God gave them over to shameful lusts. Even their women exchanged natural relations for unnatural ones. In the same way the men also abandoned natural relations with women and were inflamed with lust for one another. Men committed indecent acts with other men, and received in themselves the due penalty for their perversion.
—Romans 1:26-27

In His ultimate wisdom and authority, God created the reproductive and sexual system of human beings with the goal of sexual fulfillment in marriage and the preservation of the human race. In addition to this, He established the physical, emotional, spiritual and legal aspects that are part of this union.

> *So God created man in his own image, in the image of God he created him; male and female he created them. God blessed and said to them, "Be fruitful and increase in number; fill the earth and subdue it. Rule over the fish of the sea and the birds of the air and all the creatures that move on the ground."*
> —*Genesis 1:27-28*

The Word of God is quite clear and certain when it says that He created our sexuality. Holiness and purity characterize our sexuality, and are the seal of God's approval.

> *The man and his wife were both naked, and they felt no shame.*
> —*Genesis 2:25*

One of the consequences of man's disobedience and fall was the original sin committed by our original parents. This act contaminated the sexual relationship between the man and the woman. They were seduced by the serpent, and ate from the forbidden tree of the knowledge of good and evil. Their disobedience sentenced the human race to spiritual death. And the Word of God says that immediately following their act of disobedience, their eyes were opened and they felt shame once they saw they were naked. That which God had created pure and good for the man and the woman, had now become shameful and immoral, and had to be hidden from their eyes.

> *Then the eyes of both of them were opened, and they realized they were naked; so they sewed fig leaves together and made coverings for themselves.*
> —*Genesis 3:7*

God ordered sexual abstinence from the very creation of the world; however, there are people who are of the opinion that teaching sexual abstinence is nothing more than a desperate reaction on the part of the church to the increase in fornication among young people, and the sexual deviance that such conduct creates.

The LORD God said, "It's not good for the man to be alone. I will make a helper suitable for him."… Then the LORD God made a woman from the rib he had taken out of the man, and he brought her to the man.
—Genesis 2:18, 22

For this reason a man will leave his father and mother and be united to his wife, and they will become one flesh.
—Genesis 2:24

So they are no longer two, but one. Therefore what God has joined together, let man not separate.
—Matthew 19:6

The farther we separate ourselves from the original sexual model as intended by God, the greater the degree of sexual immorality. When people place themselves outside God's realm, their ability to descend to the lowest levels of sin and perversion will be immeasurable. Sexual deviance can result in all types of degradation, even the most inhuman and unimaginable acts for a normal person. Reality becomes distorted, and people lose all their ability to discern between good and evil.

The following is a list of some of these types of conducts and sexual aberrations:

1-Narcissism: Sexual pleasure derived from contemplation of one's own body.

2-Exhibitionism: Sexual pleasure derived from being observed by others.

3-Fetishism: Sexual pleasure derived from personal items belonging to the person loved.

4- Sadism: Sexual pleasure derived from torturing others.

5-Masochism: Sexual pleasure derived from being personally abused.

6- Necrophilia: Sexual pleasure derived from relations with the dead.

7- Incest: Sexual pleasure derived from relations with close family members.

8- Bestiality: Sexual pleasure derived from relations with animals.

9- Efebophilia: Sexual pleasure derived from relations with adolescents.

10- Pedophilia: Sexual pleasure derived from relations with children.

11-Gerontophilia: Sexual pleasure derived from relations with the elderly.

12-Adultery: Sexual pleasure derived from relations outside of marriage.

13- Hedonism: Sexual pleasure as the only purpose in a person's life.

Such lifestyles and conduct exist everywhere among all social, cultural and racial groups, and even inside the church. We must therefore remember the words of the apostle Paul to the Ephesian church:

> Put on the full armor of God so that you can take your stand against the devil's schemes. For our struggle is not against flesh and blood, but against the rulers, against the authorities, against the powers of this dark world and against the spiritual forces of evil in the heavenly realms.
> —Ephesians 6:11-12

We are involved in a life and death battle over our sexual holiness and purity. What Satan wishes to establish as moral, the church must single out as being immoral. On many occasions we may find ourselves in the wrong place at the wrong time, just like David. The kings used to go to battle during the spring,

In the spring, at the time when kings go off to war, David sent Joab out with the king's men and the whole Israelite army. They destroyed the Ammonites and besieged Rabbah. But David remained in Jerusalem. One evening David got up from his bed and walked around on the roof of the palace. From the roof he saw a woman bathing. The woman was very beautiful.
—2 Samuel 11:1-2

following the rainy season of winter in which it would have been almost impossible for the troops to travel over the muddy roads. The change in season presented an ideal moment to go to war. But the King, perhaps feeling tired from participating in so many battles and conquests, convinced himself that it was time to rest, to lower his guard, and to allow others to do his job.

His first weakness was idleness. Spiritually speaking, we should never take off God's armor and drop the Sword, which is the Word of God, because the enemy will find us in a weak and undiscerning state. David's eyes only needed one fraction of a second to fix upon his mind and heart the image of this naked woman — an event that provoked him to commit adultery.

Among the various sexual dysfunctions we encounter are problems of desire and sexual malfunction. These deviations include:

1-Homosexuality: Sexual relations with a member of the same sex.

2- Transsexualism: A change of sex.

3- Transvestism: Dressing and as a member of the opposite sex.

4- Heterosexuality: Perverted sexual relations with a member of the opposite sex.

5- Bisexuality: Having sexual relations with both men and women.

I tell you that anyone who looks at a woman lustfully has already committed adultery with her in his heart.
—Matthew 5:27

Let us examine some other commonly used terms. In previous chapters you've seen the word "fornication." The common definition is sexual intercourse between an unmarried man and woman. But does it mean anything else? The term originates from the Greek root porneia, (from which we get the word pornography). As used in the Bible, the term "fornication" refers to any sexual practice that takes place outside of marriage — not only intercourse, but also any form of sexual behavior considered to be immoral.

Even engaged couples who live together before marriage are involved in the sin of fornication. Many parents give their consent when their children are involved in pre-marital sexual activity, and even give them advice concerning safe sex. What they fail to see is that there is no such thing as safe sex. The only "safe" thing is sexual abstinence. Both living together and prostitution are a lifestyle of fornication. This term is also used in the Bible in a figurative sense, referring to apostasy and idolatry.

Some time ago we attended a continued education medical seminar for doctors with a specialty in obstetrics and gynecology. During lunch we shared a table with other colleagues. The subject being discussed was the sexual problems facing our young people and our children. One of the doctors indicated that he made sure to place condoms in the purse of his 16-year-old-daughter so that she could protect herself from contagious diseases. I noticed that for the majority of my colleagues this attitude was considered appropriate. It is modern, civilized and scientific; but it is very far away from what God says in His Word.

Pornography is the presentation of erotic conduct in books, magazines, movies, on the internet, etc., with the intent of disseminating immorality and stimulating sexual arousal. Every year, the pornography industry earns billions of dollars. Its businesses are intertwined with organized crime. Millions of adolescents begin a life of depravation and fornication after they have been seduced by pornography. Many marriages, even in Christian homes, have been destroyed when one spouse gets involved in pornography.

Maria was one of the first patients we ever saw at our practice. Throughout the years we delivered all four of her children. Here was a woman who proudly enjoyed her life, her children and her marriage. During a routine visit to the office she shared with me how concerned she felt when she found a pornographic magazine on her husband's night table. Apparently, her husband's new job had completely transformed him; his new friends and the peer pressure were beginning to change the lifestyle of this Christian man. I advised her that it was important to seek counseling from her pastor or from a trusted counselor; I was very much aware of the consequences that she and her children would be exposed to as a result of her husband's conduct and sexual aberration.

Her husband continued with his exposure to pornography to the point of becoming addicted to pornographic movies, and to buying lascivious sexual gadgets — and he made demands upon his wife to share such experiences with him. Finally this marriage ended in divorce because his sexual perversions increased over time.

Sexual abstinence is not just a simple recommendation parents make to their children so that they can stay away from sexual relations before marriage. Nor is it a method of birth control. It's a lifestyle to be practiced by every adolescent

When tempted, no one should say, "God is tempting me." For God cannot be tempted by evil, nor does he tempt anyone; but each one is tempted when, by his own evil desire, he is dragged away and enticed. Then, after desire has conceived, it gives birth to sin; and sin, when it is full-grown, gives birth to death.
—James 1:13-15

and single adult — any unmarried person who knows that God is holy, and demands that we live pure lives in order that we are not put to shame.

Most of us are aware of the issues surrounding the separation of church and state, and have seen how the Word of God has been taken out of our schools — to pray and to open a Bible in a classroom has become a crime punished by law. We have also seen how the principles of psychology (the science of human behavior) are being interpreted as absolute truth and are becoming widely accepted, even when they are completely opposed to the basic principles of morality found in the Word of God.

Early in 1996 I was participating in a *Waiting for True Love* conference in a classroom filled with about forty fourth grade students. At the request of the school counselor we dedicated a period of time to answering some of the students' questions. One question, written on a piece of paper, asked about masturbation.

In very simple terms I explained to them that it was the self-manipulation of one's sexual organs with the purpose of achieving sexual gratification or an orgasm. I shared that this was an act of self-sex, an isolated act that is selfish in character and against what God has established.

The teacher asked me to share some more about this controversial practice, because only two weeks earlier, the department of education had given a conference on this same theme. The counselor that shared with the class on that particular occasion had informed students that masturbation was necessary and therapeutic, and that it was recommended as a practice to relieve stress and to aid in strengthening the individual's sexuality.

The most disconcerting thing is that many Christian leaders also believe and teach this. Yet it is in total opposition to the teachings found in the Word of God.

There is no difference between masturbation and fornication. Like any sin, these also have repercussions and consequences that, sooner or later, will affect us. These repercussions range from a guilt complex to sexual problems that arise in a future marriage relation. Cases have been documented of individuals who became so accustomed to sexual gratification through masturbation that when

The most disconcerting thing is that Christian leaders also believe and teach this, in total opposition to the teachings found in the Word of God.

It is written: "Be holy for I am holy'"
—1 Peter 1:16

they entered into a marriage relationship they could not properly relate to the opposite sex. This is a type of severe sexual dysfunction, which may result in impotence and depression.

The sins committed against sexual holiness are an offence against God, against the purpose and dignity of man, and against humanity. Let's search the Scriptures regarding what we have learned.

Write Genesis 1:26 and explain God's concept of the creation of man.

_____

_____

_____

Lust or lasciviousness, is the uncontrolled desire for sexual satisfaction, without taking into account the reason why God created sex — for union and procreation within the legitimate bond of marriage. A lascivious person will be led to participate in sexual acts and conducts such as incest and rape, that are condemned by the laws of man.

Read the following verses and explain the spiritual condition of and the consequences faced by those who are dominated by lust.
Romans 1:26-32

_____

_____

_____

_____

Galatians 5:19-21

_____

_____

_____

_____

Ephesians 4:17-19

_____

_____

_____

I tell you this, and insist on it in the Lord, that you must no longer live as the Gentiles do, in the futility of their thinking. They are darkened in their understanding and separated from the life of God because of the ignorance that is in...their hearts.
—Ephesians 4:17-18

1 Peter 4:3-5

_____

_____

_____

In the Old Testament we find the account of Sodom and Gomorrah — a clear picture of sexual depravity that forced God to destroy both cities, but not before saving Lot and his family after his uncle Abraham intervened on his behalf.

Read the story that is found in Genesis 19:1-29 and answer the following questions.

What was the prevalent sin of Sodom and Gomorrah?

_____

_____

_____

They called to Lot, "Where are the men that came to you tonight? Bring them out to us so that we can have sex with them."
—Genesis 19:5

Who visited Lot's house? What was the reason for the visit?

_____

_____

_____

What did Lot offer the men of the city in order that they desist from their evil plans?

_____

_____

_____

What did the angels do when the men of Sodom and Gomorrah became violent?

_____

_____

_____

The main sin of Sodom and Gomorrah was homosexuality. It is from here that we take the word sodomy.

What does Jude 7 say to us?

_____

_____

_____

What type of people were the men of Sodom? Genesis 13:13

_____

_____

_____

Homosexuality is a sexual deviation in which there exists an affective -sexual relation with a member of the same sex. There are many theories as to its origin. Many people are of the opinion that it is a sickness and not a sin. Others say that it's the result of family emotional and moral disorders. Sill others say that the reasons for homosexuality are hereditary, hormonal imbalance and so on. Biblically speaking, homosexuality originates in the evil desires of man due to the sin that is produced by many social, physical, emotional, and spiritual factors.

Write the verse found in Romans 6:12.

_____

_____

_____

Summarize James 1:12-15 in your own words.

_____

_____

_____

Sexual identity is the emotional and psychological state of a human being in which he/she recognizes to which sex he /she belongs — it's a relationship between his sexual anatomy and his soul (the seat of his emotions, intellect and will).

Homosexuality begins with a lack of sexual and affective (external expression of emotion) identity by the child (boy or girl) between the ages of 6 and 12. Sexual identity is the emotional and psychological state of a human being in which he/she recognizes to which sex he/she belongs — it's a relationship between his sexual anatomy and his soul (the seat of his emotions, intellect and will).

Read the following verses and write the biblical principle present. What does God say concerning homosexuality and lesbianism?

Leviticus 20:13

_____

_____

_____

Deuteronomy 23:17-18

_____

_____

_____

_____

1 Kings 22:46

_____

_____

_____

Judges 19:22-24

_____

_____

_____

1 Corinthians 6:9-11

_____

_____

_____

1 Timothy 1:8-10

_____

_____

_____

He condemned the cities of Sodom and Gomorrah by burning them to ashes, and made them an example of what is going to happen to the ungodly.
—2 Peter 2:6

2 Peter 2:6

_____

_____

_____

Transvestism (dressing up with clothing appropriate of the opposite sex) is a sexual deviation that is not accepted by God.

Explain Deuteronomy 22:5 in your own words.

_____

_____

_____

Masturbation and self-eroticism is the act of sexually pleasing oneself. Self-arousal is an act that is offensive to God because He did not create the human body for such practices of uncontrolled sexuality. It is an act against nature because it alters the purpose of sexuality and preservation of the human race as designed by God.

What advice does God give us in the following verses?

Colossians 3:5

_____

_____

_____

Romans 6:13

_____

_____

_____

1 Corinthians 6:19-20

_____

_____

_____

1 Peter 2:11

_____

_____

_____

Read, meditate on and summarize in each verse God's plan regarding our sexuality in direct opposition to transexuality.

Genesis 1:27-28

_____

_____

_____

Genesis 2:18-24

_____

_____

_____

Mark 10:6-12

_____

_____

_____

Ephesians 5:22-25

_____

_____

_____

_____

Write what the Word of God teaches us about fornication.

1 Corinthians 6:13, 18

_____

_____

_____

1 Corinthians 7:1-2

_____

_____

_____

_____

1 Thessalonians 4:2-5

_____

_____

_____

1 Corinthians 5:9-13

_____

_____

_____

Hebrews 13:4

_____

_____

_____

Those who justify the sin of fornication in today's modern society have a reprobate and dark mind; what they don't understand is that fornication is as ancient as the devil himself — it's nothing more than old-style immorality.

Write down and meditate upon the following verses.

Romans 1:28

_____

_____

_____

Ephesians 4:17-19

_____

_____

_____

Isaiah 5:20-24

_____

_____

_____

Titus 1:15-16

_____

_____

_____

Marriage should be honored by all, and the marriage bed kept pure, for God will judge the adulterer and all the sexually immoral.
—Hebrews 13:4

The act of fornication, like any other sin, is a serious offense against God and His Word. For all who refuse to repent and seek forgiveness of their sins, and refuse to stop practicing this sin, a sentence has already been declared.

The act of fornication, like any other sin, is a serious offense against God and His Word. For all who refuse to repent and seek forgiveness of their sins, and refuse to stop practicing this sin, a sentence has already been declared. God warns us that fornication brings about eternal consequences. His wish is that we come to repentance and save our souls from eternal damnation.

Read the following verses and explain in your own words what is the end that awaits all fornicators.

Revelation 21:8

_____

_____

_____

Revelation 22:15

_____

_____

_____

God warns us about the eternal consequences of fornication so we can come to repentance and free our soul from the eternal punishment. Adultery is a sin against God and against the laws of man. It is a violation of the faithfulness covenant between a man and a woman. Summarize what the Word of God says about adultery in each of the following verses.

Leviticus 20:10

_____

_____

_____

Leviticus 18:20

_____

_____

_____

Exodus 20:14

_____

_____

_____

Proverb 6:32

_____

_____

_____

Matthew 19:18

_____

_____

_____

Romans 13:9

_____

_____

_____

Matthew 5:27

_____

_____

_____

Mark 10:11-12

_____

_____

_____

The Word of God calls sins by their true name. What is the sexual perversion that we are warned about in the following verses?

Leviticus 18:23

_____

_____

_____

Leviticus 20:15

_____

_____

_____

Exodus 22:19

_____

_____

Deuteronomy 27:21

_____

_____

Hedonism claims pleasure as its primary value and the supreme purpose in life.

Hedonism claims pleasure as the primary value and supreme purpose in life. Its proponents say that everything is allowed, as long as some level of pleasure is derived. It doesn't matter if you do drugs, steal, kill, cheat, drink, lust, etc. From a sexual perspective, hedonists view the human body as a sexual machine. Hedonism comes from the root word hedom, which means "pleasure." The Word of God condemns such philosophy that is completely opposed to God's commandments.

Write the following verses. List a few situations from your daily walk with God to which these principles could be applied.
1 Corinthians 10:23-24

_____

_____

_____

1 Corinthians 6:12

_____

_____

Humanity has a much greater love for its own desires than for God. Meditate upon the following verses and describe some of the characteristics of a hedonist.

2 Timothy 3:1-6

_____

_____

_____

Philippians 3:18-19

_____

_____

_____

The church that submits to the Word of God as its only guide in matters of faith and doctrine has been called to unmask all lies that relate to sexual deviations, by use of the truth it possesses. The Word says that God hates sin but loves the sinner, and that He came to this world to destroy the works of the devil.

Write the verse found in 1 John 3:8.

_____

_____

_____

Read the following account of a woman caught committing adultery. How did Jesus react? John 8:3-12

_____

_____

_____

_____

Answer the following questions in your own words.

What example does Jesus give to the church?

_____

_____

_____

Should we tolerate sin or preach sexual holiness? Explain.

_____

_____

_____

What would you tell a homosexual about what the Bible teaches concerning his lifestyle?

_____

_____

_____

According to the following verses, is it possible for someone with a sexually deviant lifestyle to be fully restored? Explain.

2 Corinthians 5:17

_____

_____

_____

_____

Isaiah 1:18

_____

_____

_____

_____

Jesus straightened up and asked her, "Woman, where are they? Has no one condemned you?" "No one, sir," she said. "Then neither do I condemn you," Jesus declared. "Go now and leave your life of sin."
—John 8:10-11

"Come now, let us reason together," says the LORD. "Though your sins are like scarlet, they shall be as white as snow; though they are red as crimson, they shall be like wool."
—Isaiah 1:18

Psalm 51:1-7

_____
_____
_____
_____

Micah 7:18-19

_____
_____
_____
_____

Isaiah 38:17

_____
_____
_____
_____

Romans 3:23-24

_____
_____
_____
_____

Colossians 1:12-14

_____
_____
_____
_____

God has provided a way out for those who practice sexual sin. He is the only one who can free men and women from Satan's bondage. He only asks that we recognize that we have broken His commandments and sinned against Him, that we truly and sincerely repent and follow His advice to the adulterous woman: "Go now and leave your life of sin." Such a transformation can only be guaranteed through the power of the Holy Spirit, and this is because in our own strength and will, it's completely impossible to obtain.

Write the verse found in 2 Thessalonians 2:13

_____

_____

_____

_____

When we finally recognize that as a result of our sin we are very far away from God, then Jesus intervenes and reminds us that He is the only way, and the only one who is able to renew our relationship with God and give us eternal life.

All have sinned and fall short of the glory of God.
—Romans 3:23

Write and meditate upon John 14:6.

_____

_____

_____

_____

Prayer:

Lord Jesus, we thank you for your Word because it leads to the knowledge of the truth and to real freedom from the deceptions of Satan and of this world. We ask forgiveness for all our sins, especially for every sexual, mental, or physical deviance in our lives. Thank you for saving our souls, and thank you that because you have cleansed every one of our sins with your redeeming blood, with the aid of your Holy Spirit we can now live a life that is pleasing unto you. Help us to proclaim these truths so that those who live in darkness can be brought into your saving light. Amen.

God has provided a way out for those who practice sexual sin. He is the only one who can free men and women from Satan's bondage.

Lesson 8

Disobedience and Its Consequences

You could feel the tension in the operating room. The technicians in charge of the surgical instruments were quite focused on the field of operation and were extremely attentive to every one of our words and requests. We all knew that the faster the cancer that was present in the cervix of the uterus was removed from Alicia, the better. It was a malignant cancer that was detected in the early stages and was limited to the exterior cells. But on this particular occasion we could not sacrifice quickness for the sake of safety.

We had met Alicia in our clinic for ambulatory patients at the Oncology Hospital. Three weeks after her initial visit she was already prepared for surgery. The morning on which her surgery was scheduled to take place, we had a final meeting with the surgical team to make sure that everything was in order, and prayed with them asking God to lead us during the surgical procedure.

Alicia was our first patient that suffered from AIDS and on whom we would be practicing a major intra-abdominal surgical procedure. The surgical personnel were at a high risk of exposure to the virus. The Lord glorified Himself during the procedure and everything went according to plan. Alicia was sent home after a few days without any further complications.

In ancient times leprosy, otherwise known as Hansen's disease, was considered the scourge of humanity. The infected person was easily recognized because of the gigantic ulcers that destroyed the skin, leaving the patient without fingers, nose or suffering from other disfigurement. Ancient historians wrote that people suffering from leprosy were forced to live in isolated communities, wear long robes, and even ring a bell to warn others in the street that they were passing by. These people were rejected physically, emotionally and spiritually. Some people considered lepers to be sinners that were only paying for their own sins or for the sins of their parents.

Today, leprosy is considered an affliction of the past, because there are only about two million lepers in the entire world.

If you do not obey the LORD your God and do not carefully follow all his commands and decrees I am giving you today, all these curses will come upon you and overtake you.
—Deuteronomy 28:15

Today, sexual promiscuity, the absence of moral absolutes and Christian values, and the lack of responsible sexual education in the home, churches and schools are at the forefront of society.

Today new diseases have replaced leprosy as the "scourge" of humanity.

Today, sexual promiscuity, the absence of moral absolutes and Christian values, and the lack of responsible sexual education in the home, churches and schools are at the forefront of society. To these we must add the fact that the mass media presents sex as a simple recreational pastime without any real consequences. Although we continue to repeat the facts to you throughout this study, it's vital for you recognize that young people today have been infected by bacteria that is much more dangerous than the "mycobacterium leprae" which produces leprosy. The bacteria to which we are referring is translated in a medical terminology called Sexually Transmitted Diseases (STD's). STD's include more than 60 illnesses or medical conditions produced by virus, bacteria, fungus, and different types of parasites that are transmitted by sexual relations.

In the United States, 60,000 people between the ages of 14 and 55 are infected by a sexually transmitted disease every day. Most of these are teenagers and young adults. STD's are responsible for 250 to 300 million new cases every year. If we were to calculate the number of work hours that were lost, medicines prescribed, women that are diagnosed as being sterile, children who die at birth due to contamination from the mother, others that are left disabled for the rest of their lives, young people who die, etc., we would be dealing with incalculable human and emotional loss — statistics that are so staggering our minds would not be able to handle them.

One of my patients delivered her second baby without any complications; she gave birth to a beautiful baby girl that weighed 9 pounds. One year later, during her routine medical examination, she informed me that she was having some difficulties — a foul-smelling discharge from her vagina and profuse bleeding after having sexual intercourse.

In addition to performing a Papanicolaou (test for cancer — Pap test), we checked her uterus with a special image-enhancing microscope and ordered a biopsy of the cervix. (A small sample of tissue is taken and pathology tests are done). Three days later, the medical pathologist who performed the various tests confirmed that she had an invasive form of cancer in the uterus — an extremely rare diagnosis for a young woman her age. Further investigation revealed that the cause of such a premature cancer was the human papilloma

Our young people have been infected by a bacteria that is much more dangerous than the "mycobacterium leprae," which produces leprosy.

virus; a virus that is acquired during sexual relations and that produces venereal warts in the genital area of the man and the woman.

There are many different types of this particular virus, but types 6 and 11 are highly virulent and are capable of producing cancer of the cervix in a young woman. Two weeks after the final diagnosis, an abdominal hysterectomy was performed on her (the uterus was extracted), making her unable to bear any more children.

Previously we mentioned how totally inefficient the Safe Sex campaign was. More than 3 billion dollars were spent promoting the use of condoms and oral contraceptives, in an effort to stop the high rate of pregnancy and STD's among teenagers. Today, more than 3 million young people become infected STD's every year with. Every year 1.3 million new cases of gonorrhea are reported, and it is calculated that 24 million people in the United States (especially the young) have been contaminated with the human papilloma virus.

Reliable studies have shown that nearly one million new cases of vaginal herpes are reported every year, and that nearly seventeen percent of the total population between the ages of 17 and 70 is infected. Recently it has been documented that among certain high school and college groups, the infection rate could reach as high as sixty percent.

The Safe Sex campaign was a failure; young people and their parents were deceived. They were sold the idea that protecting themselves with a condom was going to guarantee a pregnancy-free and sexually-healthy lifestyle. Yet too many young people can honestly testify that this is not true; that too many of them got pregnant; others were infected with many different STD's including AIDS; and many of them paid a heavy and dangerous price by submitting themselves to an abortion.

Maritza came to the office accompanied by her aunt, and began to describe the pain she was feeling in her genital area. At 17 years of age, she seemed not to mind that her aunt was present when she told us that she was sexually active. She described the type of lesions that had begun to appear on the outer part of her genital area. The lesions looked like pus-filled blisters. They kept the area irritated; she could hardly sit down, and above all complained of an intense, burning sensation when urinating. Without the need to examine her any further

Further studies showed that the cause of such a premature cancer was the human papilloma virus; a virus that is acquired during sexual relations and that produces venereal warts in the genital area of the man and the woman.

Today, more than 3 million young people become infected every year with STD's.

I already knew what type of STD she was suffering from. However, I proceeded with a complete pelvic exam and prescribed medication along with various laboratory tests. She was asked to return the following week.

When Maritza came to see me one week later she looked radiant, and informed me that she was completely cured. After a detailed confirmation of the lab results, I had to tell this young lady the painful truth about her condition.

She was not cured. She was only experiencing relief from her symptoms; she was suffering from an incurable disease. Genital herpes. Her beautiful smile became a heartbreaking grimace as I told her that her illness would manifest itself in recurring episodes for the rest of her life. The symptoms would appear again during periods of stress, and when her immune system was weak. The condition might reappear during menstruation or during sexual relations with a partner who is infected and the virus is in its active stage.

As doctors, we have consulted all types of literature and medical textbooks; we have reviewed our experiences as Christian medical doctors; and above all we have prayed to God in search of an appropriate treatment for these various diseases. However, our conclusion in this regard continues to be the same. We must return to the original, basic, and only plan established by God: abstinence and sexual purity, a life of sexual holiness.

We have studied a great deal of writings by individuals who defend the right to sexual freedom, safe sex, the right to privacy for our young people to do whatever they wish with their own bodies. All of their arguments have one common denominator: God has been excluded from their arguments.

You must remember that you were created in God's image, and that separated from Him there is no hope whatsoever of physical healing, emotional healing and much less any hope of spiritual healing.

That is why these sophisticated programs do not work. All the billions of dollars used in these efforts are like wood in a fireplace — money lost. As long as these people continue to exclude God from the equation and sell their failed ideas, young people will continue to die.

Recently it has been documented that among certain high school and college groups, the contamination rate could reach as high as 60%.

She was not cured. She was only experiencing relief from her symptoms; she was suffering from an incurable disease.

You must remember that you were created in God's image, and that separated from Him there is no hope whatsoever of physical healing, emotional healing and much less any hope of spiritual healing.

We recently decided to take one more look at some sophisticated research dealing with the advantages of using a condom. In a very professional and ordered fashion, the author mentioned all the statistical studies that supposedly proved that using a condom is the safest alternative available — even when compared to sexual abstinence. They are of course, wrong.

An objective analysis of this study shows that the study fails to recognize the reality of sexual promiscuity in the world. Sexual promiscuity will not be resolved with a simple conference, or by handing out latex condoms. To sponsor and promote a sexually promiscuous lifestyle is equal to setting aside all the moral values and Christian principles that were present when America was founded.

How many of these individuals do you think would be willing to recommend to their own children that they use a condom when having sexual relations with someone who has AIDS, fully trusting in the condom's effectiveness to protect?

In 1985, when I was in my last year as a resident medical student I was assigned to the internal medicine department to evaluate a 27-years-old patient named Maria. She suffered from pneumonia, as well as a recurring vaginal infection caused by a fungus called "monilia albicans." I examined the patient and confirmed the presence of the vaginal infection. Nothing else seemed suspicious…until she complained that the roof of her mouth was sore. To my surprise, I discovered that there were "monilia" lesions all over her mouth — something which is very rare in adults. Maria's boyfriend was a drug addict who had recently died in New York City, but she was unaware of the cause of his death. Maria never understood what the strange disease was she was suffering from. At the time it was not well known. But several years later Maria died of AIDS.

Sexually Transmitted Diseases –STD's

The main focus of this study is sexual abstinence, but it is necessary that we dedicate more attention to the names and symptoms of STD's, for the benefit of young people, parents and leaders. These are known as venereal diseases from the Latin word "venéreas" (belonging to Venus the goddess of love). Venereal diseases are transmitted almost exclusively through sexual contact with a person who is infected. The people that are commonly infected are young men and women between the ages of 15 and 25. The contaminated areas could very well be the sexual organs, but transmission can also occur through oral sex, anal sex, and by the hands. These infections can extend from the genital organs to other internal organs such as the prostrate, testicles, uterus, ovaries and other far away systems such as the brain and the heart.

As was previously mentioned, the organisms that produce these medical conditions are many, among which you can find more than 60 pathogens (protozoa, parasites, fungi, bacteria and viruses). Some of the more common conditions are as follow:

1- Syphilis.

2- Herpes: Type I (labial herpes) and Type II (vaginal herpes).

3- Genital warts: A virus of the human papilloma or VHP.

4- Granuloma Inguinal

5- Chancroid

6- Chlamydia

7- Cytomegalovirus CMV

8- Scabies

9- Gonorrhea

10- Lymphogranuloma venereum or LVG

11- Pubic crab louse

12- Bacterial vaginitis

13- Trichomoniasis.

14- Pelvic Inflammatory Disease or PID.

15- Urinary tract infections

16- Hepatitis

17- Molluscum contagiosum

18- Acquired Immunodeficiency Syndrome or AIDS

Each of these diseases could have many different variants which could cause it to multiply in number, which would require a larger book in order to explain each one.

The clinical manifestations and symptoms of these diseases are too many to count, but the most common are the local ones: itch; eruptions or outbreaks; blisters; swelling; foul smelling discharge from the vagina, penis, or rectum;

purulent (pussy) secretions, post-sexual intercourse bleeding, pain and burning sensation when urinating, painful sexual relations, etc.

Generalized or systemic (affecting the entire body) symptoms could be varied: unexplained loss of weight, abdominal pain, change of appetite, unexplained fever, continuous fatigue, loss of hair, mental disorders, muscular pain, vomiting and diarrhea, persistent cough, general weakness, visual problems, enlarged glands, nausea and dizziness, skin spots, loss of hearing, white spots on tongue and throat, nose bleeds, abdominal muscular strain, convulsions, etc.

> The price to pay is quite high, and the loss of physical and emotional health as a result of these conditions is irreparable.

The price to pay is quite high, and the loss of physical and emotional health as a result of these conditions is irreparable. When you listen and read about these medical conditions they seem like just another list, but there is a drastic change of scenery when it becomes personal and you are the one that must suffer one or more of these conditions in your own flesh.

An ectopic pregnancy (when the fertilized egg is detained in the fallopian tubes by some type of obstruction and the embryo begins to develop there instead of in the uterus), is one of the most feared gynecological emergencies, because there is a high risk of death for the patient involved (Illustration 3).

One young woman was admitted to the hospital with strong pains in her lower abdomen, moderate vaginal bleeding and heart palpitations. She was only in her sixth week of her first pregnancy, but all symptoms signaled a possible ectopic pregnancy. We immediately did a laparoscopy (an examination of the interior of the abdomen in which an incision is made in the navel and a special telescope called a laparoscope is inserted). In the abdominal cavity we found at least two liters of accumulated blood. During the surgical procedure that followed, we found an ectopic pregnancy in the right fallopian tube. The burst tube obligated us to remove the tube in order to stop the bleeding. (In rare cases, the tube does not break and the fetus can be observed lodged inside.) (See iIllustration 6.)

Before she was married and prior to her conversion to Christ, this young woman had suffered on various occasions from the condition referred to as pelvic swelling. Over a period of time it caused an obstruction in the right fallopian tube and was the reason she was in danger of dying.

It's very important that we analyze some of the details related to the most frequent and common of these diseases:

1—**Vaginal Herpes Type I and Type II:** Herpes is produced by a virus that, like AIDS, has no cure. This condition belongs to the group of more than 60 conditions that are acquired through sexual relations. In the last 10 years there has been a considerable increase in the number of herpes infections among high school and university students. The symptoms appear between 2 and 20 days after the person has been infected.

We used to think that this condition was related to cancer of the cervix in women, but in reality the greatest danger is for pregnant women. If during the moment of delivery there are active lesions due to Herpes Type II, a C-section must be performed; otherwise the child can become infected when he passes through the vaginal canal and die.

Usually the symptoms present are blisters that leave painful, ulcer-like lesions in the genital area. Although people might not see any apparent signs of the disease, they continue to be infected and contagious. There is no cure for this disease; the symptoms can only be temporarily relieved with antiviral drugs such as acyclovir and famcyclovir.

Herpes Type I is associated with burning sensation in the mouth and blisters around the lips.

2—**Venereal Warts:** These are produced by the human papilloma virus. There are more than 100 different types that produce a great variety of these warts. Some can cause cancer of the cervix, the vulva, and the penis. Two or three weeks after the infection has taken place, warts begin to grow in the shape of a papilla, or nipple-shaped protuberance. It can also appear as a single wart in the genital area, urinary tract, near the rectal area and mouth (Illustration 3 and 4). At times, it manifests itself as lesions or isolated warts; in the worst-case scenario, as meaty-looking warts in the shape of a cauliflower blocking the vaginal area or the anus. In order to keep the child from becoming contaminated, a C-section is performed on every pregnant patient that suffers from this condition.

A condom cannot prevent an individual from becoming infected by any of these medical conditions because the lesions that occur in different parts of the genital area are not covered by a condom.

Like herpes, this medical condition has no cure. Treatments are as varied as local surgery, laser, cryosurgery, acid applications and injections with interferon that affect the immune system.

Contrary to the postulates of the Safe Sex campaign, a condom cannot prevent an individual from becoming infected by any of these medical conditions because the lesions that occur in different parts of the genital area are not covered by a condom.

We do instruct our married patients to use a condom as an alternate method of contraception. But we are under the medical-legal obligation of explaining to you that for every 100 women that use this method, 17-18 will get pregnant. That's almost twenty percent. There are many reasons for this: The condom can break; it might have a factory defect; the wrong technique is used in wearing the condom, etc.

At the same time, the ultra-microscopic viruses can penetrate the fabric of the condom, and can even be immune to the substances used to kill the sperm, such as the chemical substance Nonoxino 19 present in the prophylactics.

In other words, using a condom is similar to playing Russian roulette; you place your life at extreme risk due to the high probabilities of becoming infected with one of these diseases.

3—Chlamydia: In the United States, this is one of the most common bacterial venereal infections among young people under 19 years of age. At least 4 million cases are diagnosed every year. It is normally associated with gonorrhea, and more than twenty-five percent of the population has both conditions. Chlamydia is the principle cause of urethritis (inflammation of the urethra) in the man, and in the woman is associated with Pelvic Inflammatory Disease. As was previously mentioned, on many occasions pelvic inflammation is responsible for an obstruction in the fallopian tubes, which is the cause of sterility in some women and ectopic pregnancy in others. Chlamydia can cause sterility in the man as well as infection of the urinary tract and epididimytis (inflammation of the internal part of the testicle).

The most common symptoms are discharge from the penis or vagina, bleeding, pain during sexual contact, and burning sensation when urinating. These symptoms can appear from 7 to 21 days after the individual has been infected; 75% of women and 40% of men do not show any symptoms once they have been infected. Part of the treatment includes the use of antibiotics and protection during the infection. During childbirth, the infected woman transmits the disease to the newborn's eyes. This can result in blindness and/or pneumonia.

4—Gonorrhea: This is a bacteria that causes sterility, arthritis and cardiac (heart) conditions. It is the main reason for many pelvic infections that can eventually result in ectopic pregnancies. Gonorrhea produces a painful discharge, in both sexes, that is yellow or green. It is associated with many urinary tract infections. The symptoms can appear 10 to 14 days after the person has been infected. The treatment consists of antibiotics for both members in a relationship.

5—Syphilis: This disease is caused by the virus treponema pallidium. It has various stages:

PRIMARY STAGE. The chancre or ulcer appears without any pain between 30 and 90 days after the individual has been infected. It appears in the genital area, lips, mouth, breast and anus. This is the contagious stage.
SECONDARY STAGE. Begins from 3 to 5 weeks after the ulcers appear; 2 years later there could be fever, fatigue, loss of hair, gland enlargement, muscle aches and skin problems especially in the hands, feet and back.
LATENT STAGE. There are no symptoms because the disease is not active. If the disease is not treated, the latent stage becomes dormant and can be the cause of many fetal abnormalities and even fetal death. Hence the importance of prenatal testing during pregnancy, and a syphilis test for couples planning to be married. The treatment most widely used is penicillin and needs continuous follow-up.
ADVANCED STAGE. Multiple body systems are affected: heart, brain, bones, etc.

6—HIV/AIDS: This is a fatal infection that is caused by the retrovirus of human immune deficiency. HIV mainly affects the immune system. It is the fifth ranking cause of death among people between the ages of 20 and 50; its final stage is the Acquired Immunodeficiency Syndrome, AIDS. The symptoms

AIDS is the fifth ranking cause of death among people between the ages of 20 and 50.

of AIDS can be observed even 10 years after the individual's infection by the HIV virus. The virus is acquired by sexual contact; by vaginal secretions; during pregnancy, childbirth or breastfeeding; sharing contaminated syringes; lesions or open cuts in the skin; and contaminated blood transfusions. It is estimated that in the United States there are close to 1 million people infected with the HIV virus, and half a million show symptoms of AIDS. The World Health Organization estimates that worldwide there are 8 to 10 million adults and 1 million children who are HIV positive.

The symptoms are varied and multiple: progressive weakness, loss of weight, bronchitis, colitis, chronic diarrhea, violet skin lesions, malign diseases due to immune problems, blood diseases, fungi, parasites, brain disorders, etc. At this time there is no known cure for the AIDS virus, but there are drugs like AZT (azidotimidina or zidovudina) which slow down the process and also lessen the symptoms as thy begin to appear.

> At this time there is no known cure for the AIDS virus, but there are drugs which slow down the process and also lessen the symptoms as they begin to appear.

The only prevention for all sexually transmitted diseases is sexual abstinence outside of marriage; without a doubt, the principle goal of abstinence is the protection of the individual and his well-being, and not the restriction of human and personal freedoms.

Now, let us search the Scriptures.

The Word of God says that all disease came into the world as direct consequence of Adam's disobedience and sin, and as a result of man's fall. In the beginning, sin and death did not exist, and all creation was subservient to man.

Write Romans 5:12

_____

_____

_____

_____

This curse extended to the whole human race. It's why we are born spiritually dead, separated from God's presence, inclined to commit evil, and with tremendous human frailties.

Explain the main idea in each of the following verses:

Psalm 14:2

_____

_____

_____

Romans 3:23

_____

_____

_____

We can safely say that sin is a disease we have inherited from our forefathers. What is the remedy for such a terrible condition experienced by human beings? Explain in your own words.

_____

_____

_____

_____

We can safely say that sin is a disease that we have inherited from our forefathers.

Study the following verses and explain what is God's plan for our spiritual healing.

Romans 5:15-19

_____

_____

_____

Scripture clearly shows that God pronounced a sentence over our bodies. What does Genesis 3:19 have to say in this regard?

_____

_____

_____

Consequently, just as the result of one trespass was condemnation for all men, so also the result of one act of righteousness was justification that brings life for all men.
—Romans 5:18

Our bodies are not immortal; they are by nature inclined toward evil, disobedience and sin. The apostle Paul refers to it as body of humiliation and body of death.

Meditate upon the following verses and write your opinion.

John 3:6

_____

_____

_____

Romans 7:21-24

_____

_____

_____

Philippians 3:20-21

_____

_____

_____

The Word says that despite our weaknesses our bodies are still the temple of the Holy Spirit.

Write 2 Corinthians 4:7-9

_____

_____

_____

_____

_____

Due to the fact that we still live in this world, we are surrounded by an environment that is sinful, hostile, and adverse to our physical and emotional well-being. Because humanity lives in a fallen world, at times we experience physical afflictions in our bodies. There are times when disease comes as a direct consequence of man's sin and disobedience.

Meditate upon the following verses and summarize each one.

Hebrews 12:3-11

_____

_____

_____

_____

1 Corinthians 11:29-30

_____

_____

_____

_____

Identify the sin and the disease that resulted.

Numbers 12:1-13

_____

_____

_____

2 Kings 5:20-27

_____

_____

_____

Numbers 21:4-9

_____

_____

_____

Psalm 107:17-20

_____

_____

_____

Deuteronomy 28:21-22

_____

_____

_____

In Mark 2:5-9 the New Testament shares an account in which Jesus was teaching that it is more important to forgive sins than to heal the body. He, of course, has the authority and the power to do both. We know that to live in sin is to be ill in our soul; our emotions, intellect and will are ill when we walk in disobedience. It has been proven scientifically that the illnesses of the soul also damage the body; that's why the forgiveness of our sin is essential to our all-around healing. The secret of a complete healing process begins with our being reconciled to God and our sins being forgiven.

Read the following verses and write verses 5, 9 and 11 from Mark 2:1-12.

_____

_____

_____

_____

_____

_____

It has been proven scientifically that the illnesses of the soul also damage the body. That is why the forgiveness of our sin is essential to our all-around healing.

There are times, such as in Job's case, when an illness is not a consequence of our sin. Its purpose is to test us, to teach us maturity and dependence upon God. Such was the case with the apostle Paul; in order to protect him from spiritual pride, he was given a thorn in the flesh. We do not know specifically what was the origin of this illness, but it is clear that it bothered his soul; his life was unbalanced and so he prayed that it be taken from him.

Read 2 Corinthians 12:7-10 and explain how God dealt with Paul.

_____

_____

_____

_____

There are times, such as in Job's case, when an illness is not a consequence of our sin. Its purpose is to test us, to teach us maturity and dependence upon God.

Summarize the main idea in each of the following verses.
Exodus 4:11

_____

_____

_____

Isaiah 43:13

_____

_____

_____

Isaiah 14:27

_____

_____

2 Chronicles 20:6

_____

_____

_____

Job 1:21

_____

_____

_____

God's sovereignty is beyond man's intellect; our finite minds will never be able to fully understand an infinite God; that is why we live by faith. Why are some healed and others are not? God is sovereign. There are times when an illness glorifies God and enhances His purposes. When Lazarus became ill, Jesus, the divine healer, received an emergency call from Lazarus' sisters. In His divine plan He answered their call, but two days later.

Read the following verses and explain Jesus' plan.

John 11:1-44

_____

_____

_____

Who received all the glory in Lazarus' illness, death and resurrection? Explain.

_____

_____

_____

What was the reaction of both sisters regarding Jesus' plans?

_____

_____

_____

In the book of Job, God gave Satan authority to touch the life of a just and fearful man. At the end of such a great test, Job arrived at a revealing conclusion. How do the following verses apply to your personal life? Do you really know God?

God's sovereignty is beyond man's intellect; our finite minds will never be able to fully understand an infinite God; that is why we live by faith. Why are some healed and others are not? God is sovereign.

Job 42:1-6

_____
_____
_____
_____

All sexual immorality brings with it disease and death: spiritual death, emotional death, and many times even physical death. Sexual abstinence outside of marriage will protect you from these diseases, from those that are still to be discovered, and those that will certainly appear in the end times.

Throughout the Bible God condemns all sexual immorality, mental as well as physical.
Explain Matthew 5:28.

_____
_____
_____

God has many personal attributes. The most popular of these is that He is love and full of mercy; but we cannot forget that He is holy and just. He will judge our daily walk, and we will receive the retribution we deserve for our sins.

All sexual immorality brings with it disease and death: spiritual death, emotional death, and many times even physical death. Sexual abstinence outside of marriage will protect you from these diseases, from those that are still to be discovered, and those that will certainly appear in the end times.

Prayer:

Heavenly Father, we present to you our weaknesses, sins and inclinations towards evil. We ask that you help us keep our bodies for your service, and that you deliver us from all physical and emotional diseases that may result from our past disobedience. Your Word stands forever, and we are aware that you have warned us concerning ancient and modern plagues. Help us to be wise and obedient, and to always be thankful for the gift of life and health. Amen.

PART TWO

Lesson 9

The Parent's Responsibility to Educate

A few years ago, a certain Catholic school suspended a 17-year-old girl because she was pregnant. The case made it to the courts because the young girl and her parents demanded their right to remain in school despite the pregnancy and her status as a future single mother. What a shameful experience it was to go as far as airing in public such immorality, and still lose the case.

I recently received a phone call from a well-loved leader, who is director of a recognized international ministry. His voice trembled as he began to cry and confess with great sadness the deep shame he felt. His only son, a child that was raised in the church and a sophomore in college, got a girl pregnant. The girl was about to give birth and he did not know what to do. The man was quite depressed as a father, and as a pastor he was asking himself if he should continue with his ministry. As I listened to him, in my heart I asked the Holy Spirit to give me words of comfort to share with this desperate father. After sharing, crying and praying together, we said goodbye to each other. And I asked myself, where did we go wrong as parents? Is there anything that we should have done, and didn't? How good is our level of communication with our children? Where have we failed to warn them? What will become of our future generations?

As parents and leaders, we must ask God to give us the ability to clearly discern and understand the times in which our young people live, a special ability that was a distinguishing mark with the members of the tribe of Issachar:

> *Men of Issachar, who understood the times and knew what Israel should do —*
> *200 chiefs, with all their relatives under their command.*
> *—1 Chronicles 12:32*

As parents, our responsibility is to instruct, train, warn and provide our children with the appropriate tools they will need to face the challenges, temptations, emotional and physical changes related to puberty, and peer pressure. This is not the responsibility of the school, or the responsibility of close relatives. It's not even the responsibility of the church. If, as children, we

Teach them to your children, talking about them when you sit at home and when you walk along the road, when you lie down and when you get up.
—Deuteronomy 11:19

didn't receive this type of instruction, we must make the decision to assume such a responsibility with our own children. We cannot continue to pass along the ignorance of our forefathers; we must be willing to break once and for all with this vicious cycle of behavior.

Even when we do fulfill our responsibility as a Christian parent, there are children out there that will rebel — they will defy the authority of their parents and then suffer tremendous consequences. As parents, we must trust and rest in God's sovereignty. However, we must not cease to be alert. We must continue to ask God to teach us. We must ask Him to burn deep in our hearts the urgency of being examples worthy of being imitated by our children, and we must effectively use the authority that He has given us. God gives us the privilege of bearing children, but at the same time He also gives us equal responsibility to properly guide them through life. From day one we must assume the responsibility before God to teach them that we are the leaders in the home and that they are the followers, not the opposite.

My son, keep your father's commands and do not forsake your mother's teaching. Bind them upon your heart forever; fasten them around your neck. When you walk, they will guide you; when you sleep, they will watch over you; when you awake, they will speak to you. For these commands are a lamp, this teaching is a light.
—*Proverbs 6:20-23*

In a family, each member has its functions and obligations. When the roles are reversed and the children begin to order their parents around, or the roles are not adequately nurtured, emotional disorders will be manifested in every member of the family, and that will result in a dysfunctional family. A dysfunctional family is outside the will of God, and if we as parents do not return to the basic principles of Scripture, we must then prepare ourselves to give account for the family He has placed under our care and authority. May God have mercy upon us.

As parents, we can bring either a blessing or a curse to our future generations. The Word of God records quite clearly the lives of men who, because of their permissive style of parenting, brought death upon their own children. This attitude characterized by passivity and tolerance toward sin produces children who are insecure, who lack the proper authority figure as a role model. For this reason these young people find refuge in inadequate leadership models, and grow up with a lack of personal satisfaction, lack of personal goals, without a vision of their worth before God, without fear and respect for authority figures, lovers of self and without natural affection, as the Word of God so clearly states. These are young people who survive in life, but do not know how to really live life; their lives lack any meaning, and as such many consider and even attempt to commit suicide.

In the first book of the prophet Samuel, chapters 1 and 5, we find the sad course of a father with a permissive character. As such he condemned his family to ruin and provoked the extinction of his whole generation. Eli, the high priest and judge, ruled over the Hebrew people during a time of spiritual decadence, yet he did not assume responsibility over his own household. The Bible introduces Eli in the latter days of his life, where it seems he had already lost the ability to discern between intoxication and genuine pain and anguish felt by a woman who begged God for a son. Such confusion on Eli's part demonstrates lack of spiritual sensitivity in listening to the Word of God, as well as poor behavior on the part of a priest. With this combination of "merits" on his side, it's quite difficult to imagine Eli as a loving father or as an effective husband knowledgeable in the dynamics and personal needs of the members of his family.

As a father I have made many mistakes. In medical school and in teaching hospitals we are trained to be good physicians, but there is no school we can attend to learn how to be good parents. All we have available to us is the schooling provided by the Word of God. This schooling will last all our lives; as our children grow and go through the different stages of their lives, we grow as well, and this by the mercy of God.

As a veteran of the armed forces I was called to active duty during the Gulf War, between 1990 and 1991. We practically set up a hospital and surgical facilities in the middle of the dessert, about 50 miles from the city of Kuwait. The military operation received the code name OJT for "On the Job Training."

In the same manner, many of the skills and lessons on how to be a good parent are acquired when the children arrive. As they grow, we continue to learn and to put into practice what God's training manual teaches us. If the Lord does not guide us, we will continuously make mistake after mistake, and our children will live a life of failure, very similar to Eli's experience with his children.

It was Hannah who made Eli realize how lacking was his gift of discernment after abandoning the counsel of God's Word and blatantly tolerating sin in his own household. At the time, women were not allowed to contradict a prophet, much less a priest. In His infinite mercy, God answered the woman's request, and Eli himself gave her a prophetic word.

Listen, my son, to your father's instruction and do not forsake your mother's teaching. They will be a garland to grace your head and a chain to adorn your neck.
—Proverbs 1:8-9

Hannah was praying in her heart, and her lips were moving but her voice was not heard. Eli thought she was drunk and said to her, "How long will you keep on getting drunk? Get rid of your wine."
"Not so, my Lord," Hannah replied, "I am a woman who is deeply troubled. I have not been drinking wine or beer; I was pouring out my soul to the Lord. Do not take your servant for a wicked woman; I have been praying here out of my great anguish and grief.
—1 Samuel 1:13-16

Eli answered, "Go in peace, and may the God of Israel grant you what you have asked of him."
—*1 Samuel 1:17*

Approximately one year later, Hannah cuddled God's promise in her arms. Her son Samuel was born, and she dedicated him to serve God in the temple, under Eli's supervision. The second chapter of 1 Samuel describes the sins of Hophni and Phineas, the sons of the priest. In verse 16 of this same chapter we can observe the spiritual decadence and corruption rampant during this time.

What happens when we neglect to invest time and effort in educating our children about the moral and spiritual aspects of the Word of God, and the reverent fear they must have toward God when dealing with sexual issues? The price we will be forced to pay due to our sin of omission and disobedience will be very high.

Miguel was a high school student with very good grades. He was well respected in his church and school because of his Christian convictions. He spoke to us about his personal struggle with an addiction to masturbation. This young man had participated in numerous conferences that dealt with the theme of sexuality, but with great feelings of resentment he shared that his father had never shared with him that masturbation was a type of fornication and a direct violation of God's holiness. He was bound physically and mentally to a particular sin, and his relationship with God had gone cold. He recognized his need for affection, and wished that his father had given him the proper guidance and information. We led him to understand that masturbation violates basic laws of God's will for our lives, and that it is a selfish sexual appetite of our flesh.

When I next saw Miguel and spoke to him, he confessed to me that victory in that particular area was his, but that he still needed to heal from the resentment and the lack of forgiveness he felt against his father.

Contrary to what many people think, the most trustworthy polls reveal that our children attempt to imitate us in every way. Many adults would think that the desire of most young people is to imitate a famous person like Michael Jordan, or perhaps some other celebrity, but such is not the case. Our genetic code and spiritual makeup does not violate the rules and norms of our Creator. The Word of God says that He created us unto his likeness, and so is the case with our

The servant would then answer, "No, hand it over now; if you don't I'll take it by force." This sin of the young men was very great in the LORD's sight, for they were treating the LORD's offering with contempt.
—*1 Samuel 2:16-17*

children. They want and need to be in their father's image. That is the way God established it.

When God comes into our lives as Lord and Savior, a miracle takes place in the spiritual realm. The Holy Spirit comes to dwell inside our lives; He convicts us of all truth, justice and sin. At that moment, a man is given one of the most important responsibilities on the face of this earth: to be a priest over his household, and responsible for the spiritual direction and sexual education of his children.

What other alternative are available to our children if we fail to exercise our duty to educate them about sexual matters? What excuses do we have not to do it? In 1 Samuel 2:29, the Lord scolds Eli on this issue. Instead of helping, leading and teaching his sons Eli honored them above God and His commandments. As a result of pleasing his sons above all, Eli's priorities in every area changed.

> *Love the Lord your God with all your heart and with all your soul and with all your strength and with all your mind.*
> *—Luke 10:27*

The sins committed by Eli's sons turned them into culprits under sentence of death. The Word of God punished their violations against God's holiness and the acts of fornication in the temple. Most shameful is the fact that Eli had known about it all along.

> *Anyone who sins defiantly, whether native-born or alien, blasphemes the Lord, and that person must be cut off from his people.*
> *—Numbers 15:30*

Eli's devotion to God came into question when he refused to punish his sons. He allowed things to remain as they were, and in the process was signing a death sentence for his household and his entire generation. The fact that he refused to speak to his sons about sexual holiness degraded his status as a priest over his own home, and over the people who trusted that he care for the tabernacle. As a result, God required that Eli be held accountable for his actions, and a death sentence was declared over his home.

Why do you scorn my sacrifice and offering that I prescribed for my dwelling? Why do you honor your sons more than me by fattening yourselves on the choice parts of every offering made by my people Israel?
—1 Samuel 2:29

And what happens to your two sons, Hophni and Phineas, will be a sign to you — they will both die on the same day. I will raise up for myself a faithful priest, who will do according to what is in my heart and mind. I will firmly establish his house, and he will minister before my anointed one always.
—1 Samuel 2:34-35

As I prayed before the Lord and meditated upon the subject matter for this lesson, I remembered the faces of my two sons Cristobal and Eduardo during a time of family devotions in which my wife Doris gave thanks to God for "every time she corrected them." They could not understand why we were so full of joy, so we read to them the prophetic word given by God to Samuel concerning the house of Eli:

> *I told him that I would judge his family forever because of the sin he knew about; his sons made themselves contemptible, and he failed to restrain them.*
> —*1 Samuel 3:13*

Satan's agenda for these end times is to bring shame over every church, family, ministry — and most of all over every young Christian man and woman as he tempts each with sexual sins. God's plan during these times is to alert parents to assume their role as priests of their household, and to teach, train and educate their children as to the beauty of sexuality and sexual abstinence. We as parents have been called to "restrain" Satan's plans.

How to Share With Our Children About Sex

What follows are some of the most frequently asked questions by parents:

1—When is the best time to speak to my child about sex?

Many years ago I visited an elementary level public school to share with children between 8 and 10 years of age. A group of about 15 students approached me as I entered the schoolyard, and one of them asked me if I was the professor that was coming to talk "fresquerias" with them. In my country, this term means to speak about sex with malice and naughtiness (slyness). When I completed my presentation, the questions from these children quickly followed. A 10 year-old girl asked the following, "My brother leaves semen over the toilet in my house and I when I sit on it I get concerned. Can I get pregnant by just being in contact with the semen?" Another one asked, "Why do you get warts on your hands when you masturbate?"

I have plenty of material to write another book about the sexual doubts and curiosities, like these, of children. But on that particular day I became convinced of something quite serious: Most of these youngsters had already developed some kind of an idea about sexuality, and in one way or another many of them had already tested them. The scary part is that their concepts were wrong, distorted, promiscuous and vulgar — quite far from biblical sexuality.

Perhaps 30 or 40 years ago, the best moment to share with our children about sex would have been once they reached puberty — in the case of boys sometime between the ages of 12 and 14, and with the girls between the ages of 10 and 13. But today, the scene has totally changed. The sexual development of our children comes much faster. It's quite common to find 9-year-old girls that have experienced their first menstruation, something which was very rare years ago. At times the accelerated physical and hormonal development is not up to par with the mental and emotional development.

Pride only breeds quarrels, but wisdom is found in those who take advice.
—Proverb 13:10

The teaching process with our children concerning their sexual development must begin at least two years prior to puberty. This teaching must be done in a systematically progressive fashion, ranging from the most elemental to the most delicate and complicated issues, as they reach the time of puberty. To wait until puberty places us at a great disadvantage in relation to the world in which they live, taking into consideration all the information they are exposed to from the mass media, movies, music, peer pressure in school, worldly lifestyles of young celebrities, the secular system of education and why not, the lack or absence of quality sexual orientation in the church.

For lack of guidance a nation falls, but many advisers make victory sure.
—Proverb 11:14

Dear parents, God is trying to tell us something; consider the education of your children as something very serious, because the abundance of evil influence from this world seeks to destroy their lives.

2—What physical changes indicate that my child has entered puberty?

Puberty is that time when an uninterrupted development in our children's sexual maturation begins. We must not forget that there are many differences between one child and the next in relation to the time and type of changes that come with adolescence. Among the many factors which contribute to such variability are genetics, nutrition, spiritual and moral factors, socioeconomic factors, physical and emotional ailments, and other unknown causes.

The production of hormones that are related to sexual development begins, in the boy as well as the girl around the age of 7. The production of estrogens is detected in girls and the production of androgens in boys.

IN BOYS:

—The redistribution and re-accumulation of the fatty subcutaneous cellular tissue begins around the hips, with a tendency to diminish as the boy grows, contrary to girls.

—Growth of the external sexual organs: testicles, scrotum and penis.

—Pubic, facial and axillary (armpit) hair becomes evident:

A discreet growth of pubic hair is observed as the testicles begin to grow. Hair turns darker in one year's period of time. In the following 2 or 3 years the hair begins to curl and extend until it reaches adult distribution.

—A change of voice begins to occur at the beginning of puberty and continues until it reaches what will be the normal tone of voice.

—The first nocturnal semen emissions begin, one year after the described changes during puberty begin — around 13 years of age.

IN GIRLS:

Once again we must say that sexual maturation changes in girls begin two years earlier than boys. It may even reach a point in which between the ages of 11 and 13 girls will be taller than boys.

—The hips and pelvis experience an evident widening.

—Mammal development: breasts begin to grow.

—Axillary (armpit) hair grows approximately one year following pubic hair growth.

—Menstruation appears two years after breast growth.

> The father should teach the boys about sex, and the mother should teach the girls.

3—Who should be the one to speak to them about sex?

We recommend that the father teach the boys about sex, and the mother teach the girls. The advantages of doing it this way are many:

—The child will feel more at ease when talking with a parent of the same sex.

—The parents could share much easier about their own struggles and doubts with the child.

—There is much greater identification and understanding by both parties when you are sharing with someone of your same sex.

—Even when the children grow, marry and leave the home the channel of communication concerning sex remains open.

—In the case of a single parent who is raising a boy or girl respectively, then professional help should be sought, such as from a professional counselor or trusted leader. We must remember that we are placing our child's sexual and intimate lives in their hands.

Read and meditate upon the following verses. In your own words, write what God commands the parents.

Deuteronomy 6:1-3

_____

_____

_____

So that you, your children and their children after them may fear the LORD your God as long a you live by keeping all his decrees and commands that I give you, and so that you may enjoy long life.
—Deuteronomy 6:2

Deuteronomy 4:9-10

_____

_____

_____

Ephesians 6:4

_____

_____

_____

Deuteronomy 11:18-22

_____

_____

_____

Psalm 78:5-6

_____

_____

_____

Proverb 22:6

_____

_____

_____

_____

Leviticus 10:8-11

_____

_____

_____

In Genesis 22:1-18 we find an illustration of the type of obedience God demands from us, and the type that we must desire. Analyze and answer the following questions:

Which other events in the life of Abraham confirmed the importance of obeying God?

_____

_____

_____

_____

Then God said, "Take your son, your only son, Isaac, whom you love, and go to the region of Moriah. Sacrifice him there as a burnt offering on one of the mountains I will tell you about."
—Genesis 22:2

Name one other important event that occurred in the life of the Hebrew people at Mount Moriah.

_____

_____

_____

What was it that God wanted to develop in Abraham's character by making such a request?

_____

_____

_____

On the way to mount Moriah something began to bother young Isaac:

> *Isaac spoke up and said to his father Abraham, "Father?" "Yes my son," Abraham replied. "The fire and wood are here," Isaac said, "but where is the lamb for the burnt offering?" Abraham answered, "God himself will provide the lamb for the burnt offering, my son." And the two of them went up together.*
> *—Genesis 22:7-8*

Looking at the way Isaac was behaving, what do you believe the relation between father and son was like?

_____

_____

_____

What was Abraham relying upon in order for God to provide the lamb for the offering?

_____

_____

_____

Mention one occasion in which God has shown you His faithfulness and trust.

_____

_____

_____

God tests our level of obedience daily; His wish is that the best that is in us will shine forth. He tests our faith and persistence in His Word. The Scriptures are clear and precise when it talks about the parents' responsibility to educate and guide their children, as well as the responsibility of the children to honor and submit to their parents.

What does the previous verse reveal about the character of God?

_____

_____

_____

The angel of the LORD called out to him from heaven, "Abraham! Abraham!" "Here I am," he replied. "Do not lay a hand on the boy," he said. "Do not do anything to him. Now I know that you fear God, because you have not withheld from me your son, your only son."
—Genesis 22:11-12

Why is it necessary that we model before our children the fear of the Lord?

_____

_____

_____

Why does the Lord refer to Isaac as "your only son" even though Abraham had another son named Ishmael with Hagar the slave?

_____

_____

_____

The story tells us that God provided a ram for the burnt sacrifice. It says Abraham *took the ram and sacrificed it as a burnt offering instead of his son.*

What principle concerning our own salvation is this passage of Scripture announcing?

_____

_____

_____

When it comes to teaching his children about sex, what is the difference between a father who knows and serves God and one who doesn't?
List the advantages.

_____

_____

_____

_____

In the following verses, what is God's command for children (sons and daughters)?
Proverbs 4:1

_____

_____

_____

Proverbs 10:1

_____

_____

_____

Proverbs 23:19-22

_____

_____

_____

Exodus 20:12

_____

_____

_____

Make a list of the sins that, according to the following verses, we must admonish our children about.

Romans 1:28-32

_____

_____

_____

2 Timothy 3:1-6

_____

_____

_____

1 Corinthians 6:13,18

_____

_____

_____

Galatians 5:19-21

_____

_____

_____

But among you there must not be even a hint of... impurity, or of greed, because these are improper for God's holy people.
—Ephesians 5:3

Ephesians 5:3-7

_____

_____

_____

Colossians 3:5-9

_____

_____

_____

1 Timothy 1:8-10

_____

_____

_____

_____

What tools has God given us to use as we instruct our children?

1 Corinthians 4:14

_____

_____

1 Thessalonians 2:10-12

_____

_____

Proverb 19:18

_____

_____

Proverb 13:24

_____

_____

Proverb 22:15

_____

_____

Proverbs 23:12-14

_____

_____

Proverbs 29:15, 17

_____

_____

Prayer:

Heavenly Father, we are thankful that we can come before Your throne of grace, and through the blood of Jesus receive mercy when we most need it. We ask your forgiveness for all the mistakes we have made at the expense of our children. Forgive the sins committed against Your Word, in the form of neglect as we attempted to raise our children. From this moment on Your Word will be the only lamp that will light our path. Amen.

Lesson 10

Showing the Way to Sexual Holiness

I was greatly impressed by Raul. He was a natural leader — spontaneous, versatile, and above all he knew how to give and follow instructions. His two years of seminary studies placed him at an advantage over the other youth his age. He had knowledge of Scripture and referred to it with decisiveness and respect. He was definitely the ideal person to lead and train the drama team that would travel with us on our next visit to Lima, Peru. I looked forward to working with him. Yet, ten months later, when I met with the organizing committee, they informed me that Raul had left the city after his girlfriend became pregnant.

Once again, the fine difference between holiness and religiosity was exposed. There are not sufficient words to alert our young people to the dangers they face, and how peer pressure affects them even in our churches. The buildings where we meet for worship, our best programs, evangelism strategies, mission work, concerts, social service efforts, and everything else we do, are by themselves not enough to help us live a life of holiness. To our God, it's more important what we are than what we do.

God created man in His own image, and as such, the original state of man was to be similar to God, to love what God loves, to think the way God thinks, and to hate what God hates. But because of the sin that we inherited from Adam and Eve, we are not born into this ideal state. We are born with a sinful nature; with an inclination toward evil, spiritually dead and separated from God; under Satan's evil lordship and authority; and under the rule of this world and our very own flesh. Many people may find this concept offensive and refuse to accept it, because in their hearts they believe that man is not "that bad;" this is however what the Bible teaches.

As we can see, all humans are led by the ways of this world. We are disobedient, and serve the pleasures and desires of the flesh. We are not born as children of love — loved by God — but as children that provoke the anger of a holy God and who are destined to God's judgment and condemnation. This reality clearly explains why there is so much social and moral licentiousness. Man lives

God did not call us to be impure, but to live a holy life. Therefore, he who rejects this instruction does not reject man but God, who gives you his Holy Spirit.
—1 Thessalonians 4:8

There are six things the LORD hates, seven that are detestable to him: haughty eyes, a lying tongue, hands that shed innocent blood, a heart that devises wicked schemes, feet that are quick to rush into evil, a false witness who pours out lies and a man who stirs up dissension among brothers.
—Proverbs 6:16-19

As for you, you were dead in your transgressions and sins, in which you used to live when you followed the ways of this world and of the ruler of the kingdom of the air, the spirit who is now at work in those who are disobedient. All of us also lived among them at one time, gratifying the cravings of our sinful nature and following its desires and thoughts. Like the rest, we were by nature objects of wrath.
—Ephesians 2:1-3

independent of God and refuses to take His Word into account, leaving himself at the mercy of Satan's rule. If this is true, it is also true that God has made a way for mankind to be completely free from this state of spiritual death and eventually return to God's intended state.

You must be born again! How can I be born again now that I am outside my mother's womb? This is the question that a Jewish teacher asked Jesus, because he didn't understand that one could be born again spiritually.

> *In reply Jesus declared, "I tell you the truth, no one can see the kingdom of God unless he is born again." "How can a man be born when he is old?" Nicodemus asked. "Surely he cannot enter a second time into his mother's womb to be born!" Jesus answered, "I tell you the truth, no one can enter the kingdom of God unless he is born of water and the Spirit. Flesh gives birth to flesh, but the Spirit gives birth to spirit. You should not be surprised at my saying 'You must be born again.'"*
> *—John 3:3-7*

God, in his abundant love, sent His son Jesus so that through His sacrifice on Calvary's cross, and the shedding of His blood, all our sins can be cleansed and we can thus be reconciled with God the Father; this way we can return to our original state of communion with Him. When Jesus comes to dwell in our hearts, we begin a new life and are attracted by His holiness. Light and darkness cannot dwell together.

> *For God so loved the world that he gave his one and only Son, that whoever believes in him shall not perish but have eternal life.*
> *—John 3:16*

This is not a religion. It is a relationship with God. A God who loves us, gives us new life here on earth and throughout eternity, gives us a new name, adopts us as His children — we belong to God's family. This process is called justification. By the grace of God we receive something that we do not deserve and can do nothing to earn it; it's a gift. The Father declares us just — free from all sin — and delivers us from eternal punishment: hell. We believe and receive this by faith in Jesus Christ. There is no religion that can save our soul; only Jesus can do that. He is the only way to the Father.

If we are ignorant of these eternal truths, we will never be able to live a life of moral and sexual holiness, which is impossible to do unless God intervenes.

There is one Person, not human but divine, who can guide us step by step toward a new birth and a life that is pleasing unto God. This is the reason He came to earth. He does not seek to exalt Himself. He seeks to glorify Jesus by bringing us to His feet to have our sins washed and to receive not only eternal life, but also the ability to live in holiness here on earth. Even when we are not aware of His presence, He will try to convince us that we are sinners in need of repentance. Once we do know Him, and He is revealed to us, we will be inseparable because we will become His permanent residency. He is our friend, counselor, strength, guide, and teacher, fountain of all truth and wisdom, and everything we need to live a life of holiness: He is the Holy Spirit.

> *The Counselor, the Holy Spirit, whom the Father will send in my name, will teach you all things and will remind you of everything I have said to you.*
> —*John 14:26*

> *When the Counselor comes, whom I will send to you from the Father, the Spirit of truth who goes out from the Father, he will testify about me.*
> —*John 15:26*

> *When he comes, he will convict the world of guilt in regard to sin and righteousness and judgment...But when he, the Spirit of truth, comes, he will guide you into all truth. He will not speak of his own; he will speak only what he hears, and he will tell you what is yet to come.*
> —*John 16.8, 13-14*

The Holy Spirit, the third person of the Trinity, will lead through a process of sanctification. This begins with the new birth and will end when we are standing before the throne of God. He will continue His perfecting work all the days of our lives.

> *Being confident of this, that he who began a good work in you will carry it on to completion until the day of Christ Jesus.*
> —*Philippians 1:6*

You are a chosen people, a royal priesthood, a holy nation, a people belonging to God, that you may declare the praises of him who called you out of darkness into his wonderful light. Once you were not a people, but now you are the people of God; once you had not received mercy, but now you have received mercy.
—*1 Peter 2:9-10*

I will put my Spirit in you and move you to follow my decrees and be careful to keep my laws.
—*Ezekiel 36:27*

Certain truths apply to all who have received Jesus as their Lord and Savior, as well as to those who the Holy Spirit is in the process of convincing to take that step of faith. We have said that we are born again spiritually, but our flesh remains unregenerate and continues to sin. The amazing difference is that those of us who have the Holy Spirit, are warned and trained to deal with this internal conflict, and are also given the biblical strategy and solution so that our sinful flesh submits itself to what the Spirit commands. Sadly enough, those who have never surrendered their lives to Jesus are still slaves to the passions and desires of their flesh, and are on the road to total destruction. How many of us have made the following statement made by Paul, a personal declaration for our Christian walk?

> *I know that nothing good lives in me, that is, in my sinful nature. For I have the desire to do what is good, but I cannot carry it out. For what I do is not the good I want to do; no, the evil I do not want to do — this I keep on doing. Now if I do what I do not want to do, it is no longer I who do it but it is sin living in me that does it. So I find this law at work: When I want to do good, evil is right there with me. For in my inner being I delight in God's law; but I see another law at work in the members of my body, waging war against the law of my mind and making me a prisoner of the law of sin at work within my members. What a wretched man I am! Who will rescue me from this body of death?*
> —*Romans 7:18-24*

The sinful mind is hostile to God. It does not submit to God's law, nor can it do so. Those controlled by the sinful nature cannot please God.
—*Romans 8:7*

In this confession we find the first step to a life of holiness:

1—Recognize that inside each of us there is a constant conflict between spirit and flesh.

Christian youth are exposed to the same temptations as other young people, but the difference is that Satan makes it look even more attractive to them. He will make them curious about pornography, and will entice them to find illicit pleasure in their dating relationships. They will be tempted to talk, dress and behave in ways that are provocative, and thus give in to fornication and other immoral conduct (alcohol, drugs, etc.). The Holy Spirit that dwells inside of them will bring the Word to mind, reminding them that they should not sow to the flesh because its fruit will eventually conquer them. With the power of the Holy Spirit they can crucify the flesh and bring it to obedience.

The sinful nature desires what is contrary to the Spirit, and the Spirit what is contrary to the sinful nature. They are in conflict with each other, so that you do not do what you want.
—*Galatians 5:17*

The blood of Jesus cannot be treated cavalierly, casually, with disrespect. You must take good care of your relationship with the Holy Spirit in order to be able to conquer temptation and not have anything to be ashamed of. The main reason we give into temptation is a lack of consecration, and that is because of disobedience to the Word of God. To be consecrated means to be set apart, separated from evil-doers and evil works, and to be completely dedicated to pleasing God. This is a lifestyle; it's life in the Spirit. The opposite of this is desecration, to damage something sacred, to participate in the same sins as the world: to be a carnal Christian. This conduct grieves the Holy Spirit. We must take heed because these are very difficult times, and giving in to the devil and his temptations can give birth to sin.

> *Submit yourselves, then, to God. Resist the devil and he will flee from you.*
> *—James 4:7*

> *Do not grieve the Holy Spirit of God, with whom you were sealed for the day of redemption. Get rid of all bitterness, rage and anger, brawling and slander, along with every form of malice.*
> *—Ephesians 4:30-31*

> *It is God's will that you should be sanctified: that you should avoid sexual immorality.*
> *—1 Thessalonians 4:3*

2—Recognize that the will of God is that we discipline ourselves and stay away from sin.

Knowing our weaknesses, how can we live in sexual holiness?

• Renew your mind: Every day you must identify the lies of the world and the devil, and replace them with the truth of the Word of God.

> *Do not conform any longer to the pattern of this world, but be transformed by the renewing of your mind. Then you will be able to test and approve what God's will is — his good, pleasing and perfect will.*
> *—Romans 12:2*

• Occupy yourself in spiritual things that help you grow: prayer, discipleship, study of the Word of God, church participation, spiritual seminars, etc.

The one who sows to please his sinful nature, from that nature will reap destruction; the one who sows to please the Spirit, from the Spirit will reap eternal life.
—Galatians 6:8

Those who belong to Christ Jesus have crucified the sinful nature with its passions and desires.
—Galatians 5:24

I have been crucified with Christ and I no longer live, but Christ lives in me. The life I live in the body, I live by faith in the Son of God, who loved me and gave himself for me.
—Galatians 2:20

The mind of sinful man is death, but the mind controlled by the Spirit is life and peace.
—Romans 8:6

• Guard your body that is the temple of the Holy Spirit, and refuse to expose it to the temptations and sins of this world. Christian young people who have paid the price of sexual holiness enjoy many enviable blessings.

They aren't exposed to sexually transmitted diseases.

They don't live according to peer pressure.

They aren't exposed to unwanted pregnancies.

They don't suffer from emotional disorders as a result of sexual sins.

They have no need to interrupt their future plans and goals.

They live in healthy harmony with God, parents, their church, and peers.

They will have healthy marriages: spiritually, physically and emotionally.

They will be good witnesses to other youth.

They will be recognized as people of integrity and moral responsibility.

They will sow respect and order into the lives of their children and grandchildren.

Is there a second chance for those who have been involved in sexual immorality? Yes. A second virginity is available for those who wish a change of life and want to live a life of sexual holiness, not because of remorse but out of genuine repentance. God, who searches the heart, knows what our real intentions are; He cannot be deceived.

The sacrifices of God are a broken spirit; a broken and contrite heart. O God, you will not despise.
—Psalm 51:17

I the LORD search the heart and examine the mind, to reward a man according to... what his deeds deserve.
—Jeremiah 17:10

If you are already a Christian, the Holy Spirit convicts you and takes you to a place of reconciliation with God. Study the Word of God diligently; pray without ceasing; stay away from those things that will cause you to be tempted. Your priorities must change. If you have never asked Jesus to forgive you and to come and live by His Spirit in your life, then this could be your moment of decision. He wants you to separate yourself from the evil things of this world. He wants you to become His child, and to begin to live a life of holiness.

Prayer:

> *Lord Jesus, I recognize that I have lived outside of Your will. I have sinned with my body and with my mind. Please forgive me. Restore my life, deliver me from evil and cleanse me so that I may experience a renewal and a second virginity in holiness. May your Holy Spirit give me the strength and power that I need. Amen.*

Now, let's search the Scriptures.

According to Romans 6:12-13, what advice does the apostle Paul give to the Roman church in relation to its moral and sexual behavior?

_____

_____

_____

Using this same verse but in your own words, what would you say to a young person concerning sexual holiness?

_____

_____

_____

According to Romans 12:1-2, how can we know the will of God?

_____

_____

_____

What must we do with our bodies?

_____

_____

_____

What is the name given to individuals who do not take God into account and live morally and sexually disordered lives? Summarize the main idea in each of the following verses.

Psalm 14:1

_____

_____

_____

Psalm 10:4

_____

_____

_____

Psalm 53:1-4

_____

_____

_____

What is God's command in each of the following verses?

1 Peter 1:14-16

_____

_____

_____

_____

2 Corinthians 7:1

_____

_____

_____

What do the following verses tell you?

1Peter 14-16

_____

_____

_____

Leviticus 11:44

_____

_____

_____

Since we have these promises, dear friends, let us purify ourselves from everything that contaminates body and spirit, perfecting holiness out of reverence for God.
—2 Corinthians 7:1

Leviticus 19:2

_____

_____

_____

The world is in darkness. It has been prophesized in Scripture, and we experience it daily. Modern generations give witness to this fact; people today are far from God, they live independent from biblical authority, and they are unaware of the prohibitions contained in God's moral law. They are at the mercy of the evil powers and principalities of this world.

Write 1 John 2:16-17:

_____

_____

_____

What three sources of evil are offered by the world?
1._____
2._____
3._____

Where do they come from?

_____

_____

When everything has passed away, what is the only thing that will remain?

_____

_____

Only the Word of God will produce holiness in our lives. The Word exposes the lies and teaches the truth; it gives freedom; it heals; and it prospers and shows the way to sexual holiness. Millions of believers live under this truth, and it has protected them from all sexual immorality.

Summarize 2 Peter 1:19-21.

_____

_____

_____

Why is this word given by the prophets certain?

_____

_____

_____

Why must we pay attention to it?

_____

_____

_____

What is the purpose of the Word?

_____

_____

_____

> The Word exposes the lies and teaches the truth; it gives freedom; it heals; and it prospers and shows the way to sexual holiness.

Write Hebrews 4:12-13.

_____

_____

_____

Explain why the Word must separate the soul with all our emotions, our intellect, and our will from the things of the Spirit.

_____

_____

_____

The Word will judge our actions, and we will give account of everything that is exposed.

Explain Jeremiah 17:9-10 in your own words.

_____

_____

_____

Our own hearts can lie to us and take us down the road of immorality. Observe the ways of Christian young people once they get to college. The truth is, when they leave for college, a large percentage of young people fall away from the truths of the Bible and allow themselves to be seduced by the world-system.

List three reasons why university students fall away from the biblical truths they once held dear.

1._____

2._____

3._____

Name possible situations in which the Word of God is opposed to the desires of the heart. Use scripture to back up your statement.

_____

_____

_____

_____

_____

_____

The Word will judge our actions, and we will give account of everything that is exposed.

How does a life of holiness become a reality in our lives?
John 17:17

_____

_____

_____

God wants us to return to the original state of creation and to develop a close communion with Him. The knowledge and study of His Word produces holiness in our body, mind and spirit. It drives us away from immorality, sin and disobedience. Meditate on 2 Peter 1:4 and write the main truth.

_____

_____

_____

_____

What does God want us to participate in?

_____

_____

_____

_____

How do we participate?

_____

_____

_____

_____

A life of holiness is a life of close communion with the Holy Spirit. To enjoy His fellowship means to please Him in everything we think, say and do. In exchange for our desire to obey Him, He allows us to enjoy His person and enjoy His fruit. The Bible talks about the singular fruit of the Spirit, because it is one Holy Spirit with multiple virtues which express the work He has produced in us.

Write Galatians 5:22.

_____

_____

_____

_____

What are the virtues of the Holy Spirit that control your life? Explain.

_____

_____

_____

_____

What are the virtues which still do not manifest themselves in your life and why?

_____

_____

_____

_____

All of the virtues of the Holy Spirit are equally important in order to live a moral and sexually holy life. Let's examine specifically the fruit of self-control as it relates to immorality and sexual abstinence. When we talk about self control we are talking about being your own boss; about resisting peer pressure; about bringing the appetites of the flesh with all its passions and desires under the dominion of the Word of God; about subjugating your impulses; about doing what God demands rather than what you want; about not making any decision contrary to Scripture; about being sober and not giving in to impulses. It means that you decide to abstain. To have self-control is to live a life of holiness.

Write 1 Corinthians 6:12.

_____

_____

_____

What things or situations could be considered as legitimate or permissible but not beneficial or convenient? Explain.

_____

_____

_____

_____

Summarize 1 Peter 4:3-5.

_____

_____

_____

Sexual holiness is a commandment received from God. Many might laugh at our decision to remain pure, but this was already foretold. We will be blessed because the Word of God will find its fulfillment in us.

Prayer:

Heavenly Father, thank you for the power of your Word and the work of the Holy Spirit in our lives. Our holiness rests upon the blood of Christ and in Your faithfulness. Every day that goes by we want to be more like You. Help us persevere in purity, love your Word, and confess our weaknesses. Amen.

Sexual holiness is a commandment received from God. Many may laugh at our decision to remain pure, but this was already foretold. We will be blessed because the Word of God will find its fulfillment in us.

Lesson 11

Talking About Sexual Holiness from the Pulpit

And he said to me, "Son of man, eat what is before you, eat this scroll; then go and speak to the house of Israel." So I opened my mouth, and he gave me the scroll to eat. Then he said to me, "Son of man, eat this scroll I am giving you and fill your stomach with it." So I ate it, and it tasted as sweet as honey in my mouth.
—Ezekiel 3:1-3

In 1966, one year after we began the Waiting for True Love ministry, we received an invitation from a church to come and share with 300 students and their parents about sexual abstinence. The attendance surpassed our expectations. When the youth pastor welcomed us, his hands were sweaty and he had a distressed look about him. Obviously, not everything was going according to plan. He immediately pulled us aside and asked us to consider eliminating the visual illustrations: anything dealing with childbirth, the C-section, the reproductive systems and everything related to the issue of abortion.

I could not hide my total surprise when he explained the reason for his request. Church elders were present who might become offended. With as much love and understanding as we could, we explained to the young pastor the need of the 300 students and their parents to know the truth, and to confront the real issues dealing with their sexuality.

We opened the Bible and shared how the Lord called everything He created with His hands "good." Thus, we told him, we could not declare that something created by His own hands is mundane. With the help of the Holy Spirit, he became convinced of the great need to communicate this information, and with the help of the Holy Spirit he felt at peace with what we were about to do that evening.

At the end of the conference I challenged the students to make a covenant of sexual abstinence, and they quickly came forward. The presence of the Lord was manifested in a very real and special way, to the extent that even many single adults expressed their desire to keep themselves pure for the Lord. To our surprise, the elders of the church were the first people to approach us and express their gratitude to God for His work among the students. A few of the ladies invited us to speak to the married couples, since two cases of incest had been identified in that same congregation (sexual relations among family members).

Dear brothers and sisters, God has allowed us to walk hand in hand through the pages of this book. We have prayed daily that God will shine His blessing over your life and allow you to continue growing in His Word, and above all, to understand that to preach about sexual abstinence and sexual purity is a divine commandment. With the same devotion we teach about salvation, we must also accept the challenge He extends to the church to teach and preach about the reality of sexual holiness for these end times.

In the same manner that Ezekiel ate the written Word, symbolizing by this act the total acceptance of God's Word, the Church must preach everything that has been written from Genesis to Revelation. Of one thing we can be sure; God will call us to accountability and will ask us what we did with the Word He entrusted into our hands.

From the moment the Lord revealed to us the theme for this chapter, we felt a mixed sense of fear and expectation as to how the Holy Spirit would guide us. However, something was very clear in our hearts. We, the church of Christ, have evaded talking about the subject of sexuality as if it were totally excluded from God's Word. Many people have decided that this subject matter is to be discussed outside of the church, because according to our religious criteria, it's not "spiritual." Many think we shouldn't even talk about it in our homes. How very far are we from the truth and from the heart of God!

The lips of a priest ought to preserve knowledge, and from his mouth men should seek instruction — because he is the messenger of the LORD Almighty.
—Malachi 2:7

Can we blame our young people when they search for answers to their sexuality in the world, in pornography, in secular movies, from their friends or with boyfriends and girlfriends? Are we going to continue with such puritanical attitudes that we allow their lives to be destroyed? We must assume the position God has given us, because we have the truth that can deliver them from spiritual and physical death. We are the messengers of God's Word.

Many of us have fallen into the trap that considers the subject of our sexuality immoral, depraved, or the degenerate side of the human race. Because we have yielded our authority to inform, educate, train, and alert the people of God, the world system has taken complete advantage and enthroned itself in every aspect of society, including churches. Our young people easily yield to the immoral offers of this world, offers that contaminate everything created and approved by God, even human sexuality. In the book of the prophet Hosea, chapter 4, God admonishes our grave error and sin of omission.

My people are destroyed from lack of knowledge. Because you have rejected knowledge, I also reject you as my priests; because you have ignored the law of your God, I also will ignore your children.
—Hosea 4:6

This admonishment is quite clear and serious, and it should lead us to bow down and beg God's forgiveness.

And now, dear children, continue in him, so that when he appears we may be confident and unashamed before him at his coming.
—1 John 2:28

We have the word of the prophets made more certain, and you will do well to pay attention to it, as to a light shining in a dark place, until the day dawns and the morning star rises in your hearts.
—2 Peter 1:19

Only the Word of God is able to provide knowledge and freedom from the sexual sin to which our young people, single adults and even married couples are bound.

How can a young man keep his way pure? By living according to your word.
—Psalm 119:9

The church of the new millennia has to adjust its strategies to the post-modern world in which it lives. There is still some kind of taboo in most homes concerning the subject of sex. The technological advances and the great inventions in the field of communication in this twentieth century have not been able to lift the veil of apprehension that exists when parents and children talk about their sexuality, even within the confines of our homes.

Then you will know the truth, and the truth will set you free.
—John 8:32

Our churches have not been exempt from this lack of communication; we've been made to believe that the subject of sex does not belong in the pulpit because it represents a direct attack up the holiness of the pulpit. And as sin marches up the steps of our church buildings, and even occupies a seat at the altar, we refuse to listen to the cries of our youth as they become so very lost due to a lack of wise counsel.

Today many marriages are so dysfunctional — because they, too, have tremendous sexual problems — that they won't even show one single sign of positive response despite long hours of counseling. Our heavenly Father, in His infinite love and wisdom, has equipped the church with a multiplicity of gifts for very specific purposes. These are not gifts meant for the entertainment of the person who received them. They are given to be used correctly and responsibly in aiding others.

It was he who gave some to be apostles, some to be prophets, some to be evangelists, and some to be pastors and teachers, to prepare God's people for works of service, so that the body of Christ may be built up.
—Ephesians 4:11-12

The pastors and the teachers have been entrusted with sharing the prophetic Word to the church, for the specific purpose of perfecting and building up the people of God. As such, the Word must be taught and preached in its entirety, including issues that relate to sexuality. The pulpit must bring forth light, beauty, peace, security, holiness, trust, freedom and above all holiness, to the subject of human sexuality.

All Scripture is God-breathed, and is useful for teaching, rebuking, correcting and training in righteousness.
—2 Timothy 3:16

Many years ago a good friend of mine who is a pastor commented that he felt insecure and without the proper tools when it came down to discussing sex with his people. He wasn't sure what to tell a young man who had many doubts about his own sexuality. He felt quite uncomfortable in talking about the sin of fornication. He didn't know how to confront the issue of several young ladies in the church who had become pregnant outside of marriage.

My friend finally recognized that he was not pastoring and protecting the sheep in his congregation. They were being trampled by sexual immorality. He admitted his need to ask for forgiveness, first to God, and then to his congregation. He wanted to be trained, to be able to bring his knowledge up to date in order to be a true blessing and not a stumbling block to the members of his congregation.

Times have changed. Young people today demand answers. The story of the birds and the bees is passé — not even appropriate for pre-school children anymore. Adults also need, and wait to receive from their pastor, the best orientation available. The time for drinking milk is over; Christians need solid and nutritious food that will prepare them for their roles as priests in their homes. The subject of sexuality is the least-preached and talked about of all subjects, yet at the same time it is responsible for many of the sins within the

Then I will give you shepherds after my own heart, who will lead you with knowledge and understanding.
—Jeremiah 3:15

I will place shepherds over them who will tend them, and they will no longer be afraid or terrified, nor will any be missing, declares the Lord.
—Jeremiah 23:4

155

church. Our concern and worry about the frequency of sexual sin in the pastorate should alert us as to the need to know and teach about sexuality. Our position as leaders does not make us immune to Satan's stalking.

In the book of Ezra we read about the action taken by a leader as he was confronted with the sin of the people. The people were admonished and instructed to resolve such grave a situation. They had committed spiritual fornication and were involved in unequally yoked marriages.

> *After these things had been done, the leaders came to me and said, "The people of Israel, including the priests and the Levites, have not kept themselves separate from the neighboring peoples with their detestable practices, like those of the Canaanites, Hittites, Perizzites, Jebusites, Ammonites, Moabites, Egyptians and Amorites. They have taken some of their daughters as wives for themselves and their sons, and have mingled the holy race with the people around them. And the leaders and officials have led the way in this unfaithfulness.*
> —*Ezra 9:1-2*

The marriage of the sons of Israel with women from pagan tribes was totally prohibited by God. Violating this amounted to an abomination before the Lord. The purpose of such a law was to keep the people of Israel from being contaminated with the idolatry and the cults to other gods. Ezra recognized his responsibility to denounce it, and to lead the people to repent and ask God's forgiveness for such an abominable sin. As their spiritual leader, he assumed a radical position in order to honor the Word of God. He not only denounced the sin, but assumed part of the blame along with the people. He identified himself as a sinner and called upon God's mercy.

Four biblical principles serve as the foundation to teach about sexuality from the pulpit:

1. Recognize, accept and treasure the unconditional and divine call to teach the whole counsel of God, including sexuality — exalting the purity and holiness of the Lord. In addition to this, we must discern what sins of immorality are present in the church.

Keep watch over yourselves and all the flock of which the Holy Spirit has made you overseers. Be shepherds of the church of God, which he bought with his own blood.
—*Acts 20:28*

When I heard this, I tore my tunic and cloak, pulled hair from my head and beard and sat down appalled.... And prayed "Oh my God, I am too ashamed and disgraced to lift up my face to you, my God, because our sins are higher than our heads and our guilt has reached to the heavens."
—*Ezra 9:3, 6*

In the presence of God and of Christ Jesus, who will judge the living and the dead, and in view of his appearing and his kingdom, I give you this charge Preach the Word; be prepared in season and out of season; correct, rebuke and encourage — with great patience and careful instruction.
—2 Timothy 4:1-2

The church at Corinth had a problem with sexual immorality. The goddess Aphrodite or Venus was the center of worship. More than one thousand prostitutes served in her temple. In his first letter to the Corinthians, the apostle Paul openly admonished them concerning their sexual immorality, specifically singling out the sin of incest and fornication.

It is actually reported that there is sexual immorality among you, and of a kind that does not occur even among pagans: A man has his father's wife.
—1 Corinthians 5:1

In the book of Leviticus, this practice was condemned in the Hebrew laws.

Do not have sexual relations with your father's wife; that would dishonor your father.
—Leviticus 18:8

Paul admonished the Corinthians because the leaders had tried to deal with this sin in a lighthearted manner.

You are proud! Shouldn't you rather have been filled with grief and have put out of your fellowship the man who did this?
—1 Corinthians 5:2

We firmly believe in the restoration of those who have fallen due to sexual immorality, but how will they be able to rise up without someone to preach to them?

2. Recognize that our authority is from the knowledge of the Word of God and from the wisdom and guidance of the Holy Spirit.

Ezra was recognized as a scribe priest and a great leader. He was commissioned by the King of Persia himself to lead the second expedition to reconstruct the

You are sent by the king and his seven advisers to inquire about Judah and Jerusalem with regard to the Law of your God which is in your hand…And you Ezra, in accordance with the wisdom of your God, which you possess, appoint magistrates and judges to administer justice to all the people of Trans-Euphrates — all who know the laws of your God. And you are to teach any who do not know them.
—Ezra 7:14, 25

walls of Jerusalem. But his main role was being a servant of God and someone who knew God's Word. This was so evident that even a pagan king like Artaxerxes recognized and accepted his leadership, knowledge and obedience to the Word of God.

Against the Word of God there is no valid argument; the opinion of humanists and philosophers changes with time and according to what the people wish to hear. Our principles of sexual morality are eternal because the Word is eternal.

> *The grass withers and the flowers fall, but the word our of God stands forever.*
> —*Isaiah 40:8*

3. Recognize that we are part of the body of Christ and that we need to seek training and counsel when necessary from mature and qualified believers, whenever we are facing problems of sexual immorality in the church.

Every pastor must recognize his need to surround himself with a group of spiritual men and women who have knowledge of Scripture, who are disciplined in their prayer life and who use their gifts to help him pastor efficiently and care for all the needs of his congregation.

> *The things you have heard me say in the presence of many witnesses entrust to reliable men who will also be qualified to teach others.*
> —*2 Timothy 2:2*

4. Recognize that our testimony of moral and sexual integrity is our outmost representation before God and the church.

Unfortunately we have all witnessed the ways in which many men and women of God have been swept by the same sexual sins they once condemned from the pulpit. No one is free from the temptations of the flesh, but we have the Holy Spirit on our side to help us deny ourselves daily.

> *"Those who belong to Christ Jesus have crucified the sinful nature with its passions and desires. Since we live by the Spirit, let us keep in step with the Spirit."*
> —*Galatians 5:24-25*

Now the overseer must be above reproach, the husband of but one wife, temperate, self-controlled, respectable, hospitable, able to teach, not given to drunkenness, not violent but gentle, not quarrelsome, not a lover of money. He must manage his own family well and see that his children obey him with proper respect. (If anyone does not know how to manage his own family, how can he take care of God's church?)
—1 Timothy 3:2-5

In his first letter to the Corinthians, the apostle Paul expressed himself in the following way:

> *Now to the unmarried and the widows I say: it is good for them to stay*
> *unmarried, as I am. But if they cannot control themselves, they should marry,*
> *for it is better to marry than to burn with passion.*
> —*1 Corinthians 7:8-9*

The apostle Paul could speak with authority about sexual abstinence, because besides being knowledgeable in Scripture, his preaching was backed up by a life of holiness and sexual purity. In summary, the theme of holiness and sexual purity is a life and death issue for the church. It must be preached, taught and ministered from the pulpit because Scripture orders it. Our responsibility is not just to teach, but also to heal and restore those who have been victimized by sexual immorality.

The great majority of young people today live without a defined set of goals for their lives. Many say that they do not really know what they want out of life, they don't know what to study, they do not trust in anyone, and are not completely sure that their parents love them. And if they visit a church, many of them are simply that, a visitor. They do not understand themselves and never consecrate themselves to God's service. Their main worry is their appearance and to enjoy the moment. They expose themselves to all the pleasures and temptations offered by Satan and the world.

Unfortunately, many of the young people that belong to our churches share these same characteristics; with the exception that maybe they have a greater participation in Christian activities. If they are not taught that their compass in life should be the Word of God, and that in the Word they will find the answer to all of their needs — physically and emotionally, including their sexual life — our purpose as a church will have failed.

Let us search the Scriptures. Write and analyze the following verses.
Psalm 119:105

_____

_____

_____

_____

The theme of holiness and sexual purity is a life and death issue for the church.

Proverb 6:23

_____

_____

_____

Proverb 22:6

_____

_____

_____

Ephesians 6:4

_____

_____

_____

God has given us, as biological and spiritual parents, the great responsibility to raise our voices in a sound of warning, and to establish the guidelines that they are to follow in order for their lives to make sense, and avoid being accountable for a tragedy.

What was ordered and promised to young Joshua?
Joshua 1:7-8

_____

_____

_____

_____

Summarize the following verses.
Deuteronomy 5:32-33

_____

_____

Deuteronomy 4:39-40

_____

_____

_____

> God has given us as biological and spiritual parents, the great responsibility to raise our voices in a sound of warning, and to establish the guidelines that they are to follow in order for their lives to make sense, and avoid being accountable for a tragedy.

Ephesians 1:17-18

_____

_____

_____

We the leaders, with the aid of the Holy Spirit, must do what is necessary to evoke a love of Scripture among our youth, and more important, obedience to commandments; they will then become men and women of wisdom who cannot be manipulated by ignorance.

Read Proverbs 2 and summarize the benefits of understanding and wisdom, and the dangers these will help you to avoid.

_____

_____

_____

Throughout this book we have mentioned what some might consider controversial issues about sexuality, along with verses to back up our points. There is no doubt that next to the parents, we, the spiritual leaders of the church have the responsibility to unmask Satan's lies, and to speak God's truths. This is an issue we must manage with decisiveness and not superficially.

What were the accusations leveled against the priest's of Israel?
Jeremiah 6:14

_____

_____

_____

Read Ezekiel 34:1-10.
What were the character traits of the sheep?

_____

_____

_____

Who are the wild animals of our day?

_____

_____

_____

We the leaders, with the aid of the Holy Spirit, must do what is necessary to evoke a love of Scripture among our youth, and more important, obedience to commandments; they will then become men and women of wisdom who cannot be manipulated by ignorance.

Why were the sheep scattered?

_____

_____

What warning is given in the following verses?
Acts 20:29

_____

_____

Matthew 7:15

_____

_____

2 Timothy 3:1-6

_____

_____

List the character traits of those whom God has called to ministry.
Titus 1:6-9

_____

_____

_____

We are engaged in a war between what is truth and what is not, and we are the defenders of truth. We must be willing to demolish all confusing arguments that relate to sexuality and sexual abstinence.

Summarize 2 Corinthians 10:3-6 in your own words.

_____

_____

_____

Today's church is similar to the city of Jerusalem during Nehemiah's time. When Nehemiah and Jews from the captivity returned to Jerusalem, the city was in ruins, without walls and without doors. All the enemies had free access and could come and go as they pleased. They would enter the city to cause fear with all kinds of lies. The people were defenseless and unprotected. When they prayed, they were quick to recognize that sin had taken over their bodies.

Write and meditate upon Nehemiah 1:3-8.

_____

_____

_____

Answer the following questions about the previous verses:

_____

_____

_____

List the actions he took once he received the news.

_____

_____

_____

As leaders, we must know how to approach God in prayer. Read and analyze the verses found in Nehemiah 1:6-11 that record Nehemiah's prayer.

What basic elements were included in his prayer?

_____

_____

_____

_____

Today's church is similar to the city of Jerusalem during Nehemiah's time.

What leadership traits can we find in Nehemiah 1:6-7?

_____

_____

_____

_____

As pastor or leader, you must pray to the Holy Spirit for the gift of discernment, knowing that every good gift comes from the Father. This will make you able to discern the strategies of the enemy among the congregation, and equip the people to remain steadfast in their desire for sexual holiness. Nehemiah prepared himself with fasting, prayer and humiliation before he went to present his case before his boss, King Artaxerxes.

Analyze Nehemiah 2:2-8 and answer the following questions.

What was Nehemiah's job and position in the palace of King Artaxerxes?

_____

_____

_____

Why was it that Nehemiah could not present himself before the king with a sad face?

_____

_____

_____

As pastor or leader, you must pray to the Holy Spirit for the gift of discernment, knowing that every good gift comes from the Father. This will make you able to discern the strategies of the enemy among the congregation, and equip the people to remain steadfast in their desire for sexual holiness.

What were Nehemiah's three requests before Artexerxes?

1._____

2._____

3._____

Write and meditate upon Nehemiah 2:17.

_____

_____

_____

_____

What were the conclusions reached by Nehemiah? What did he decide to do in order to bring restoration to the people of God?

_____

_____

_____

_____

Dear leaders, too often we have allowed for the walls of God's truth found in Scripture to be weakened and even demolished. Young people are searching for a place where they are secure, and protected from the word and from Satan's lies and deceit. Our churches, and specifically parents and spiritual leaders, are called to protect them from evil and from their own wicked inner desires. We must build a wall of protection around them, free from fear and condemnation. We must construct walls of sexual holiness. This sexual holiness must be guarded in our churches, because the enemy will use every single act of carelessness to harm and destroy what the Word has taught them.

What was Nehemiah's decree against the enemies of Jerusalem?

_____

_____

_____

_____

What should be our decree?

_____

_____

_____

_____

Our churches, and specifically parents and spiritual leaders, are called to protect them from evil and from their own wicked inner desires. We must build a wall of protection around them, free from fear and condemnation. We must construct walls of sexual holiness.

What did Nehemiah do to protect the people from being contaminated by their enemies? Nehemiah 7:1-3

_____

_____

_____

_____

Explain what must we do in order to protect our youth from sexual immorality.

_____

_____

_____

_____

The Word of God is the Sword of the church; it's our offensive weapon against Satan's lies about sexuality. Many times we make the mistake of working too much in the church, but are careless with those who attend the church.

Explain the main idea in Hebrews 4:12-13.

_____

_____

_____

_____

_____

_____

Prayer:

Heavenly Father, we worship and honor your name. Help us to be servants according to your own heart and the leaders that the church needs in these last days. Place within us, as you did with the sons of Issachar, the ability to discern the times and its opportunities. We pray for the gift of discernment and sensibility to the voice of your Holy Spirit. Give us passion for your Word; train us, and allow us to speak with boldness. We ask for self-control. Keep us from sinning and from offending your holy name. We wish to be pastored by you, so that we in turn may pastor your sheep. Thank you for the love, patience and mercy you have extended to each of us. Amen.

Lesson 12

Sexual Purity and the Holiness Covenant

It was a wonderful evening. December 11 of 1999 had finally arrived and the Christian and Missionary Alliance Church in Aibonito, Puerto Rico was having a great celebration. The radiant couple, Johnny Rivera and Natalia de la Texera walked down the aisle to join their lives in the holy bond of matrimony.

When the couple was about to exchange wedding ring, the parents of both couples approached the altar. Both Johnny and Natalia returned to their parents the rings they had received from them as part of an abstinence covenant four years earlier.

This meant that the couple had remained virgins for each other. They had realized, accepted, lived and believed that it pays to wait for true love. Only the two of them and the Lord knew that they had been faithful to the sexual purity covenant, and the day of their wedding celebration was the right moment to make it public. The place was filled with a deep sense of solemn holiness.

Most of the adults present who witnessed that scene were overcome with profound emotions, and asked the Lord in silence that this same scene be repeated with their own children. The adolescents and youth were also witnesses of the resounding testimony that abstinence and sexual purity is possible, it's real and it pleases God.

The young couple from the church, whose ministry was to teach sexual holiness to the youth, was now enjoying the fruit of their labor, which would surely be followed by God's spiritual reward.

The word covenant comes from the Hebrew word *berit,* and appears in the Old Testament more than 280 times. The word is used to designate treaties, deals and arrangements between two parties, governments or countries with the intent of a mutual benefit. Another word from the Greek *diateke* is also used, and it is translated as alliance or testament. A covenant is a mutual agreement between two parties. Two different types of covenant appear in the Bible: the covenants made between men or nations and the covenants made between God and man.

I will make a covenant of peace with them; it will be an everlasting covenant. I will establish them and increase their numbers, and I will put my sanctuary among them forever. My dwelling place will be with them; I will be their God, and they will be my people.
—Ezekiel 37:26-27

I will establish my covenant with you, and you will enter the ark — you and your sons and your wife and your sons' wives with you.
—Genesis 6:18

In the Word of God we find many different types of covenants, starting with the covenant God made with Noah. The agreement was that before and after the flood, God would guarantee his life and that of his family. A second agreement was that God would not use a flood again to destroy the earth. As a sign to this agreement God placed a rainbow in the sky.

> *Whenever the rainbow appears in the clouds, I will see it and remember my covenant between me and you and all living creatures of every kind.*
> *—Genesis 9:16*

God is faithful, and has kept every single one of His words. The covenants have a divine and perpetual guarantee on God's part. We however, are unfaithful, and quickly forget what we have promised. Still, He remains faithful.

In the summer of 1997 we had the opportunity to visit the country of Panama. For one whole week a team of 26 people and myself offered abstinence conferences in schools and churches. One Sunday we were invited to minister in one of the largest local churches in Panama City, a building that resembled a stadium, where thousands met. When the altar call was made in which I emphasized the sexual purity covenant, we were astonished to see more than one thousand young people fill the area around the altar and down the church aisles. Many of the young people cried as they repented of their sin. This was undoubtedly an unforgettable moment for us and for them.

How many of these young people had truly offered their lives to God in an act of consecration and abstinence? If you are reading these pages and you are a young person, a parent or a single adult, one thing you need to realize is that there is a great need for a life of holiness and that the sexual abstinence covenant is not an agreement between people.

> *When the sun had set and darkness had fallen, a smoking firepot with a blazing torch appeared and passed between the pieces.*
> *—Genesis 15:17*

This verse confirms the covenant between God and Abraham, which is another one of the many covenants described in Scripture. As part of a Hebrew custom, animals were sacrificed and cut in half; then the parties involved in the covenant

I tell you the truth, until heaven and earth disappear, not the smallest letter, not the least stroke of a pen, will by any means disappear from the Law until everything is accomplished.
—Matthew 5:18

It is easier for heaven and earth to disappear than for the least stroke of a pen to drop out of the Law.
—Luke 16:17

If we are faithless, he will remain faithful, for he cannot disown himself.
—2 Timothy 2:13

walked through the middle of both pieces as a sign that the agreement was sealed. On this occasion, only God, in this case symbolized by a blazing torch, walked between the pieces, meaning that this was His covenant and that He was responsible for it.

The only guarantee that the abstinence covenant has is that God is the first party and we are the second party involved. Our commitment is not with another person, churches, doctrines, parents, pastors, leaders, the government, doctors, and psychologists or with ourselves, but with God. And it's guaranteed, because at the moment of temptation the Holy Spirit is present and if you listen attentively to His voice, He will show you the way out.

We trust in God and in His promises. It's impossible for a human being to live a life of holiness unless God Himself is involved in such a life. Our responsibility is to love and study the Word, to know God's moral ethic, to flee from sin and to desire holiness in our lives. Only when we are totally dependent upon God and reverently fear Him, will we be able to guarantee such a life. The success of sexual purity and the abstinence covenant depends on our commitment to remain in Him and in His Word.

> *I am the vine; you are the branches. If a man remains in me and I in him, he will bear much fruit; apart from me you can do nothing.*
> *—John 15:5*

Blessed is the man who perseveres under trial, because when he has stood the test, he will receive the crown of life that God has promised to those who love him.
—James 1:12

In previous chapters we mentioned that Joseph's covenant of holiness and obedience was with God. When faced with temptation Joseph was able to run because he refused to sin against God, against his master and against his own body. Had God not been his main priority, perhaps he would have given in to temptation. Read Joseph's words:

> *No one is greater in this house than I am. My master has withheld nothing from me except you, because you are his wife. How then could I do such a wicked thing and sin against God?*
> *—Genesis 39:9*

In the chapter about the parent's responsibility to educate we clearly established that parents are responsible before the Lord to share with their children about

No temptation has seized you except what is common to man. And God is faithful; he will not let you be tempted beyond what you can bear. But when you are tempted, he will also provide a way out so that you can stand up under it.
—1 Corinthians 10:13

this subject. The abstinence covenant will result in a double blessing when it is confirmed between the child and the parents.

1—At what age should we talk with our children about the abstinence covenant?

As soon as we observe signs of puberty we should begin planning a special conversation with them about their sexuality and God's holiness. The sexual education process begins at an early age — we must constantly sow in our children the moral and spiritual values that will shape their character and personality. Because of the changing times, we must be looking to identify that special time when we can talk with them about holiness and sexuality. We cannot take the chance that our children receive this valuable information from the wrong people.

Many years ago a friend of mine who is president of a particular denominational group was summoned to the United States with the intent of resolving a very delicate situation in one of their new missions that was meeting in a home. A 6-year-old girl had begun behaving quite strangely and refused to go the meetings in that home. With great wisdom and discernment, the child's mother asked her to explain what was wrong. Since she suspected that the issue was sexually related, she gave the girl two dolls of the opposite sex. To her surprise, the child placed the dolls in the oral sex position.

Ten unsupervised children between the ages of 8 and 10 had found a pornographic magazine in the bedroom of the teenager that lived in the home where the meetings took place. There was very little my friend could do to fix the tragic situation. The feelings of shame, the accusations between the members of the group, and the irreconcilable differences that resulted from this hidden sin ended the life of this young congregation.

2—How do we establish an abstinence covenant with our children?

Whatever method you choose to use should be based upon a healthy relationship of trust and love with your children. Your efforts will have as much effect as any of the many conferences they are exposed to in school. In order to have such a conversation with them, you need to have a good rapport and friendship with them. You must recognize the individuality and personality of each child, and be able to effectively recognize their needs in order to properly focus the conversation on their sexuality.

When the time to speak finally arrives, an atmosphere of expectancy must be created — the father with the boys and the mother with the girls. You must let them know ahead of time what the theme of the conversation is going to be, and you should prepare yourself in prayer to answer any questions they might have. It's necessary to study human anatomy and the human reproductive system. Otherwise you may experience some embarrassment if your children knew more than you about it. Many parents hide behind the fact that they lack the appropriate knowledge, and transfer this responsibility to other members of the family, to the church or to a schoolmate. The price you pay for this grave error is too high. Instead, when faced with questions you cannot answer, you must make the commitment to search for one.

Once you have shared this information with your children you can be sure you have established a new channel of communication with them. Your children will begin to see you in a different light. You will have earned their confidence and you will be like a good friend with whom they can share their intimate concerns.

It's fundamental that you search the Scriptures, and that they support everything that you share with your children.

3—Where should the covenant take place?

Some churches enjoy the blessing of having a sexual abstinence orientation program as part of their ministry for their youth. After a few weeks of orientation, they hold a ceremony in which young people sign the covenant before their parents, and the congregation then ratifies the agreement. Even when this is the method used, you must remember that the parents are the ones who should begin the initial conversation with them.

An alternative is to invite your son or daughter to a dinner in a comfortable restaurant, where you can then share privately with them and seal the covenant with a prayer. You might also decide to prepare a special dinner at home and then introduce the subject. That is the way we chose to do it with our sons Cristobal then 9, and with Eduardo then 12. The place you choose is not as important as the fact that God is the main guest and the One who seals this covenant. We cannot hide or diminish God's demands concerning holiness and sexual purity. He is the one who validates and authenticates the covenant.

4—What symbol should we give our children to seal the abstinence covenant?

We gave our children a chain with a key-shaped pendant hanging on it, which represented the key to their heart. The symbol that is most often utilized is a simple silver ring. In our conferences we hand out a certificate containing the abstinence covenant, which is signed by the young person and by us. The pastor of the church or any other authority figure is asked to sign as a witness.

5—What are the advantages of signing an abstinence covenant?

I will make you into a great nation and I will bless you; I will bless you;
I will make your name great.
—Genesis 12:2

Because of this oath, Jesus has become the guarantee of a better covenant.
—Hebrews 7:22

God gave Abraham three very specific promises: He would make Abraham into a great nation, He would bless him, and make his name great. God is fully committed to the covenants in which He participates. It's part of His nature and part of His perfect plan. The redemption of our sins is based on the promise by which He gives of Himself through His Son Jesus.

You yourselves have seen what I did to Egypt, and how I carried you on eagles' wings and brought you to myself. Now if you obey me fully and keep my covenant, then out of all nations you will be my treasured possession. Although the whole earth is mine, you will be for me a kingdom of priests and a holy nation.
—Exodus 19:4-6

In the covenant with Moses, God also became bound by His Word. In this particular covenant, He guaranteed the position of Israel over other nations, and as His chosen people: *out of all nations you will be my treasured possession.* God is committed to, and guarantees the covenants He makes with His children.

6—The benefits of signing an abstinence covenant before the Lord.

1—It has the support and guarantee of the Word of God.

2—In the process we are recognizing our sins, begging for forgiveness and reconciling ourselves with Him.

If we walk in the light, as he is in the light, we have fellowship with one another, and the blood of Jesus, his Son, purifies us from all sin. If we claim to be without sin, we deceive ourselves and the truth is not in us. If we confess our sins, he is faithful and just and will forgive us our sins and purify us from all unrighteousness.
—1 John 1:7-9

3—The Holy Spirit comes to dwell in our heart and we begin a process of sanctification.

4—He will give us the strength to withstand when we are tempted by fornication, adultery, lust, masturbation, etc.

5—We will be a testimony to all.

6—We will keep our bodies free from STD's.

7—By being pure when we reach the altar, our marriage relationship will rest upon the solid rock of holiness and purity that belongs to the Lord.

8—The possibility of a divorce is drastically reduced among couples that are virgins on their wedding might.

9—Our faithfulness to God blesses our children and all future generations.

10—If we sin and sincerely repent, He will restore us.

> *"Let us then approach the throne of grace with confidence, so that we may receive mercy and find grace to help us in our time of need."*
> *—Hebrews 4:16*

7—Can a person who is not a virgin sign a covenant of abstinence?

When we genuinely repent, God's forgiveness is complete and absolute. We believe in the concept of a *second virginity*. The concept of virginity is much more than an issue of anatomy and hymen integrity. It's a spiritual concept. As physicians we are constantly asked to confirm if a person has been physically violated. The anatomy, strength and elasticity of the hymen vary from one woman to the next. Certain hymens are so elastic or resistant they can only break during vaginal childbirth. If that woman has had children by C-section, and we use the term virginity in a purely anatomical context, then we must say that this married woman with children is a virgin.

The Samaritan woman (the woman at the well) had many reasons to go to the well in under the noontime scorching heat. She had quite a bad reputation due to her licentious lifestyle, and perhaps did not wish to meet with anyone. She was surprised by this Jewish man who asked her for some water and did not seem to mind that she was a woman from the town of Samaria. The Lord spoke to her about obtaining living and eternal water, and about true worship of God. When He confronted her and pointed out her life of fornication, she believed Jesus, accepted Him and preached about her encounter with Him. She went from being a sinner to being a preacher; only an encounter with God's holiness could have resulted in such transformation. She was given the gift of a second virginity — Jesus gave her a new opportunity.

Many of the Samaritans from that town believed in him because of the woman's testimony, "He told me everything I ever did..." They said to the woman, "We no longer believe just because of what you said; now we have heard for ourselves, and we know that this man really is the Savior of the world."
—John 4:39, 42

8—How can we make sure that our children remain faithful to the covenant?

On our trip to the Dominican Republic, during one of the evening conferences, a group of about ten girls waved a paper they were each holding in their hands in front of us. At the end of the evening they approached us and produced the abstinence covenant they had signed four years earlier. They had come to the conference with the intention of renewing their decision before the Lord.

We have experienced the painful truth of young people who commit to the covenant and then fall into fornication as they are seduced by the world. They must surely repent of their sin. A true believer and true child of God cannot involve himself in a lifestyle and practice such as this.

King David wanted to fulfill the covenant he had once made with his friend Jonathan. Neither the passing of time, nor the death of his friend could invalidate such a promise; the covenant was eternal, and as such David would care for and protect the descendants of Jonathan. If men can establish such a high level of commitment with each other, why can't we commit in the same way with God?

> *"Do not ever cut off your kindness from my family — not even when the LORD has cut off every one of David's enemies from the face of the earth." So Jonathan made a covenant with the house of David.*
> *—1 Samuel 20:15-16*

It is our duty as parents and leaders to intercede in prayer for our children, so that they can remain strong and continue to be faithful to the sexual abstinence covenant. We must be effective in our communication with them, be their friend and counselor, and encourage them through difficult times.

9—Who should sign the covenant?

From the time our son Eduardo signed the covenant in 1994, he has kept it hidden in a safe place, and every so often he shows it to us and puts it back in its place. Some young people frame it and proudly hang it up in their bedrooms, while others given it to their parents or to their pastors. We recommend that you allow your child to do whatever works best; and this also goes to other singles that sign the covenant.

"Do not ever cut off your kindness from my family — not even when the LORD has cut off every one of David's enemies from the face of the earth." So Jonathan made a covenant with the house of David.
—1 Samuel 20:15-16

At the end of this book there is a copy of the certificate that is ready to be signed by the student and by a witness. If you have never made this covenant part of your life, and after reading this information the Holy Spirit leads you to do so, then don't hesitate to sign it. God wants to protect you. Take the page with the certificate out of the book and sign it before the Lord. Then, when you find the man or woman of your dreams, give it as a gift to the person you are marrying, as a living testimony of consecration before God for such a special moment as this.

Let us search the Scriptures.
Write and meditate upon the verses found in Genesis 6:6-7.

_____

_____

_____

What was God's motive for such a decision?

_____

_____

_____

Are there are any similarities between this event and the parable of the prodigal son in Luke 15:11?

_____

_____

_____

Ours is a God of covenants. He is faithful to keep His word; the miracle of our salvation is precisely the foundation for the New Covenant or New Testament. From Genesis to Revelation we find many different covenants that were made between men and between God and man.

Read and meditate upon Genesis chapter 9 then answer the following questions.

What covenant is mentioned in this chapter? Write it in your own words.

_____

_____

_____

_____

Ours is a God of covenants, and He is faithful to keep his word; the miracle of our salvation is precisely the foundation for the New Covenant or New Testament.

Which sign guarantees this covenant?

_____

_____

_____

_____

The Word of God says the following in Genesis 6:8, "*Noah found favor in the eyes of the Lord,*" and this in light of the fallen nature that will accompany us until the final redemption of our bodies. Noah made one fatal mistake with fatal consequences. Read Genesis 9:21-25. What was Noah's fatal mistake?

_____

_____

_____

_____

_____

The Word of God says the following in Genesis 6:8, *"But Noah found favor in the eyes of the Lord,"* and this, in light of the fallen nature that will accompany us until the final redemption of our bodies. Noah made one fatal mistake with fatal consequences.

What 3 words of advice would you have given Noah in order to avoid such an incident?
1._____
2._____
3._____

Scripture condemns getting drunk.

> *Nor thieves nor the greedy nor drunkards nor slanderers nor swindlers will inherit the kingdom of God.*
> —*1 Corinthians 6:10*

Write 3 reasons why a person that has entered into a covenant should refrain from getting drunk.
1._____
2._____
3._____

Throughout Scripture we read about the many different reasons why God enters into covenants with man. We are not worthy of any special favors from God, but He, in His infinite mercy, finds pleasure in blessing us and in continuing with

His plan to redeem the world and to use us as earthly and imperfect vessels to show forth His promises.

In your own words write the motive behind the following covenants.

Genesis 12:2

_____

_____

_____

_____

Genesis 28:20-22

_____

_____

_____

_____

Exodus 19:5-8

_____

_____

_____

_____

2 Samuel 7:1

_____

_____

_____

_____

Nehemiah 9:38

_____

_____

_____

_____

Read and meditate upon the verse found in Genesis 17:10. Answer the following questions.

We are not worthy of any special favors from God, but He, in His infinite mercy, finds pleasure in blessing us and in continuing with His plan to redeem the world and to use us as earthly and imperfect vessels to show forth his promises.

What was the requirement for that covenant?

_____

_____

_____

_____

Who were included in that covenant?

_____

_____

_____

_____

The sexual abstinence covenant has a common denominator with the covenant previously described: the principle of obedience. When we realize this principle, will have a guide to keep us from falling and from placing ourselves in dangerous situations. In the same sense, when we are lacking in self-control or patience, we become vulnerable to Satan's plans and strategies.

Write and meditate upon the verse found in Genesis 16:1-2.

_____

_____

_____

_____

What reasons motivated Sarai to make this decision?

_____

_____

_____

_____

What were the immediate negative results?

_____

_____

_____

_____

What were the future negative results?

_____

_____

_____

_____

Now we are under a new covenant and Jesus Christ is our mediator. What are some of the traits of he New Covenant? Read and meditate upon Hebrews 8:7-13.

_____

_____

_____

_____

Now we are under a new covenant and Jesus Christ is our mediator.

Summarize Romans 8:38-39 and write what they mean to you personally.

_____

_____

_____

_____

Is this New Covenant Eternal? Explain.

_____

_____

_____

_____

Who guarantee this covenant? Hebrews 7:22, 25

_____

_____

_____

The blood of Jesus opened the way to the Father, and it allows us to sit in heavenly places; this is why we consider ourselves as aliens and strangers in this world. The Holy Spirit sanctifies us daily, protecting our identity as children of the Most High God. The New Covenant safeguards and confirms the sexual abstinence covenant.

Because of this oath, Jesus has become the guarantee of a better covenant.
—Hebrews 7:22

Dear friends, I urge you, as aliens and strangers in the world, to abstain from sinful desires, which war against your soul.
—1 Peter 2:11

Prayer:

Heavenly Father, I thank you for the privilege of studying your Word. I realize that You have all authority in heaven and in earth. The truth is only found in You. I wish to commit, seal and consecrate my life to Your service. My desire is to be pure because this is what You demand, and because You are pure. By faith, and being aware that the power of the Holy Spirit will keep me in sexual holiness, I will sign this sexual abstinence covenant. It's only a piece of paper, but to me it is significant because it represents a covenant of love with You; it will be etched in my heart forever. Thank you for loving me so much and for providing all that is necessary for my protection and salvation through the precious blood of Jesus. Amen.

Ilustrations

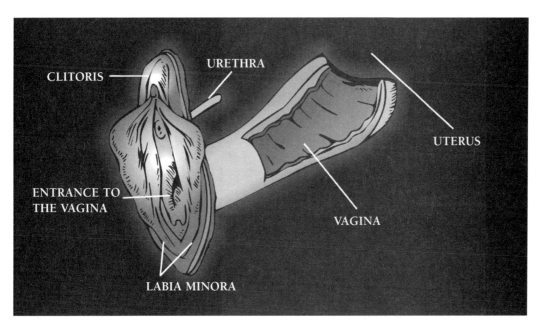

Figure 1
Female genitalia.

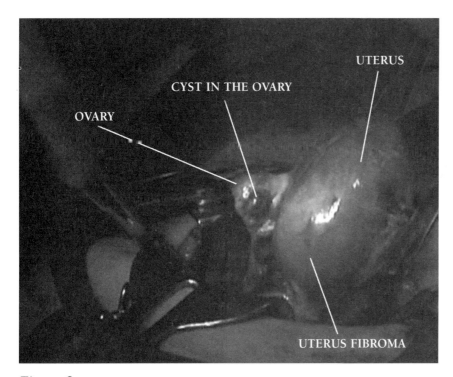

Figure 2
Patient with an ovary cyst.

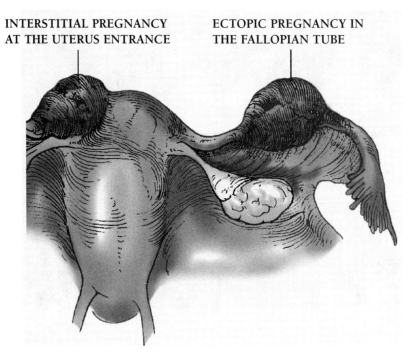

Figure 3
Ectopic pregnancy.

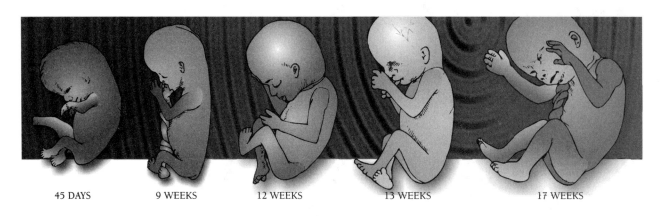

| 45 DAYS | 9 WEEKS | 12 WEEKS | 13 WEEKS | 17 WEEKS |

Figure 4
Fetus at different ages.

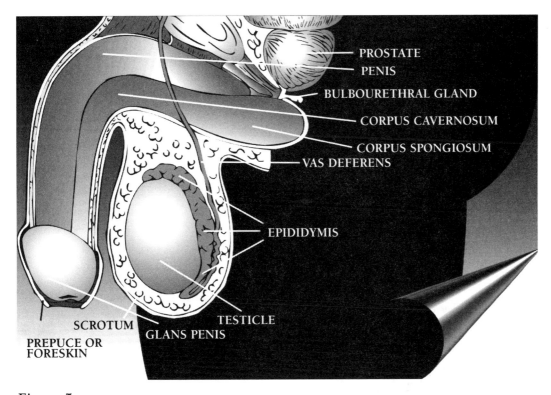

PROSTATE
PENIS
BULBOURETHRAL GLAND
CORPUS CAVERNOSUM
CORPUS SPONGIOSUM
VAS DEFERENS
EPIDIDYMIS
TESTICLE
SCROTUM
GLANS PENIS
PREPUCE OR
FORESKIN

Figure 5
Male genitalia.

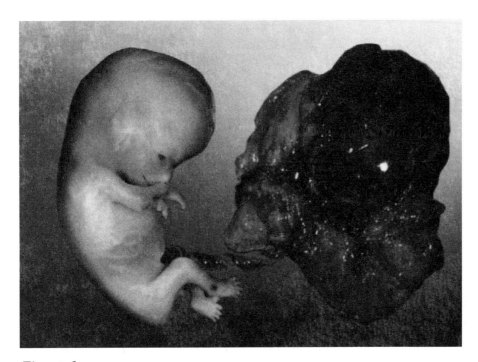

Figure 6
Ectopic pregnancy with a 44 day fetus.

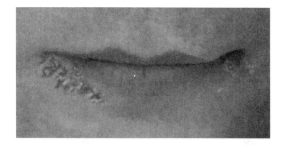

Figure 7
Papilloma virus on the lip (AIDS patient).

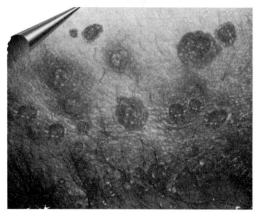

Figure 8
Genital herpes type II.

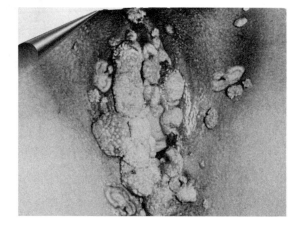

Figure 9
Human Papilloma virus.

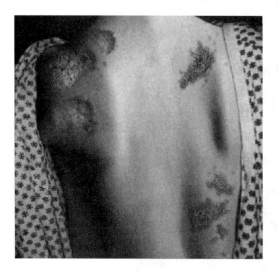

Figure 10
Back lesions produced secondary to
syphilis on an AIDS patient.

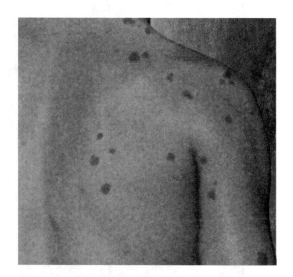

Figure 11
Sarcoma de Kaposi on an
AIDS patient.

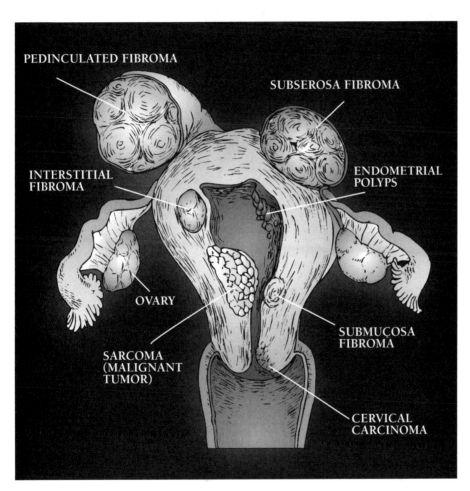

Figure 12
Benign and cancerous tumors in the uterus.

Figure 13

THE DELIVERY
Newborn on the mother's abdomen.

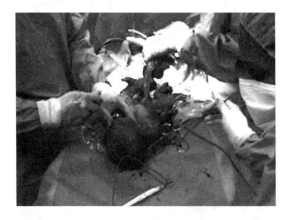

Cutting the cord.

Taking care of the baby.

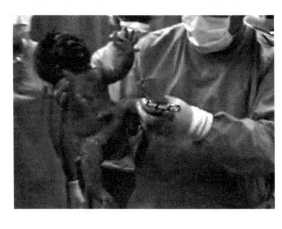

OBGYN doctor checking out the baby.

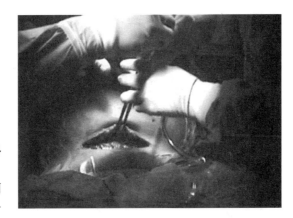

Figure 14

THE CESAREAN OPERATION
Cutting the abdomen.

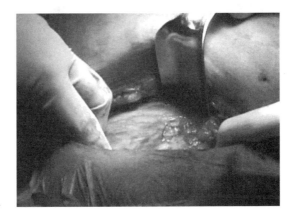

The uterus.

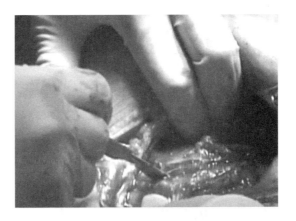

Cutting the uterus muscle.

Baby's head.

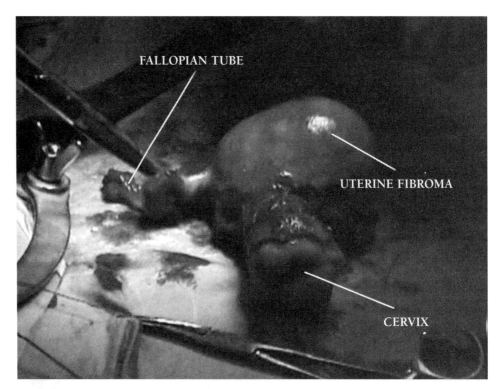

Figure 15
Removed uterus.

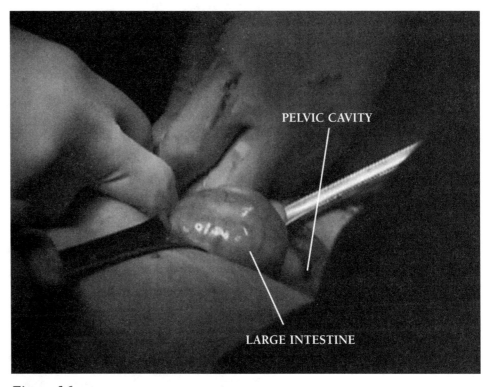

Figure 16
Anatomic relation between the intestine and the pelvis.

Abstinence Covenant

It is God's will for me to be sanctified; to avoid sexual immorality; to learn to control my own body in a way that is holy and honorable, not in lustful passion like those who don't know God. It is also God's will that in this matter of sex I don't wrong others or take advantage of them. I know that He did not call us to be impure, but to live a holy life. Therefore, I understand that when I reject this instruction I'm not rejecting man but God, who gives me his Holy Spirit.

I know that all other sins I commit are outside my body, but when I sin sexually I sin against my own body. I know, too, that my body is a temple of the Holy Spirit, who is in me, whom I have received from God. I know this means I am not my own; I was bought at a price. Thus, I should flee from sexual immorality. I should honor God with my body. I should strive always to keep my conscience clear before God and man.
(Based on 1 Thessolonians 4:3-8;1 Corinthians 6:18-20; Act 24:16)

In the light of the above truths, forgetting what lies behind, reaching forward to what lies ahead, and with the intent of allowing God to make my sexuality and my life all He wants it to be, I make this covenant before men and God that from this day forward, by the Grace of God:

—I will mirror His image
—I will seek the divine purpose for which God has created me and I will complete His plan for my life
—I will establish a legacy of godliness for my generation, my family, my seed and the generations of my family that follow me
—I will keep myself pure and a vessel of honor. I will abstain from sexual intercourse and all activities that would arouse improper desires in myself, and all others
—I will wait for marriage and live a life of sexual purity until God releases me to the person he would lovingly choose to be my spouse

Today, I make this pledge and step into divine purpose and destiny. Old things are passed away and all things have become new.

Signed by my hand this_____, day of_____

Name:_____

Witnessed by : _____

Real Problems... Real People... Real Life... Real Answers...

THE INDISPUTABLE POWER OF BIBLE STUDIES

Through the Bible in One Year
Alan B. Stringfellow • ISBN 1-56322-014-8

God's Great & Precious Promises
Connie Witter • ISBN 1-56322-063-6

Preparing for Marriage God's Way
Wayne Mack • ISBN 1-56322-019-9

Becoming the Noble Woman
Anita Young • ISBN 1-56322-020-2

Women in the Bible — Examples To Live By
Sylvia Charles • ISBN 1-56322-021-0

Pathways to Spiritual Understanding
Richard Powers • ISBN 1-56322-023-7

Christian Discipleship
Steven Collins • ISBN 1-56322-022-9

Couples in the Bible — Examples To Live By
Sylvia Charles • ISBN 1-56322-062-8

Men in the Bible — Examples To Live By
Don Charles • ISBN 1-56322-067-9

In His Hand
Patti Becklund • ISBN 1-56322-068-7

In Everything You Do
Sheri Stout • ISBN 1-56322-069-5

7 Steps to Bible Skills
Dorothy Hellstern • ISBN 1-56322-029-6

Great Characters of the Bible
Alan B. Stringfellow • ISBN 1-56322-046-6

Great Truths of the Bible
Alan B. Stringfellow • ISBN 1-56322-047-4

The Trust
Steve Roll • ISBN 1-56322-075-X

Because of Jesus
Connie Witter • ISBN 1-56322-077-6

The Quest
Dorothy Hellstern • ISBN 1-56322-078-4

God's Solutions to Life's Problems
Dr. Wayne Mack & Nathan Mack • ISBN 1-56322-079-2

A Hard Choice
Dr. Jesús Cruz Correa & Dr. Doris Colón Santiago
ISBN 1-56322-080-6

11 Reasons Families Succeed
Dr. Richard & Rita Tate • ISBN 1-56322-081-4

Rare & Beautiful Treasures
Nolene Niles • ISBN 1-56322-071-7

Love's Got Everything To Do With It
Rosemarie Karlebach • ISBN 1-56322-070-9

Problemas reales... Gente real... Vida real... Respuestas reales...

EL INDISCUTIBLE IMPACTO DE LOS ESTUDIOS BÍBLICOS

A través de la biblia en un año
Alan B. Stringfellow • ISBN 1-56322-061-X

Preparando el matrimonio en el camino de Dios
Wayne Mack • ISBN 1-56322-066-0

Mujeres en la Biblia
Sylvia Charles • ISBN 1-56322-072-5

Parejas en la Biblia
Sylvia Charles • ISBN 1-56322-073-3

Decisión Difícil
Dr. Jesús Cruz Correa y Dra. Doris Colón Santiago
ISBN 1-56322-074-1